M000159415

Expert Advisor Programming

Creating Automated Trading Systems in MQL for MetaTrader 4

Andrew R. Young

Edgehill Publishing

SECOND PRINTING

Copyright © 2010, Andrew R. Young. All rights reserved.

Published by Edgehill Publishing, Nashville, TN.

Disclaimer of Warranty: While we have strived to ensure that the material in this book is accurate, the publisher bears no responsibility for the accuracy or completeness of this book, and specifically disclaims all implied warranties of of merchantability or fitness for a particular purpose. Neither the author nor publisher shall be liable for any loss of profit or any other non-commercial or commercial damages, including but not limited to consequential, incidental, special, or other damages.

"MetaTrader 4," "MQL" and "expert advisor" are trademarks of MetaQuotes Software Corp.

This book and it's publisher is not in any way endorsed by or affiliated with MetaQuotes Software Corp.

For more information on this book, including updates, news and new editions, please visit our web site at http://www.expertadvisorbook.com/.

ISBN: 978-0-9826459-0-1

Table of Contents

Introduction

The foreign exchange market has rapidly become one of the most popular markets to trade in recent years. Because of its round-the-clock hours, high leverage and low margin requirements, thousands of ordinary people have become active traders.

MetaTrader 4 (commonly abbreviated as MT4) has become one of the most popular trading platforms for forex. Developed by MetaQuotes Software Corporation, MetaTrader is offered by hundreds of forex brokers worldwide, including big names such as GAIN Capital, FXCM, Alpari and Interbank FX.

MetaTrader's popularity stems from the fact that it's free, broker supported, and includes many useful technical analysis tools. But probably the biggest reason for MetaTrader's success is the powerful MQL programming language.

MQL has made it possible for traders to program their own custom indicators and automated trading strategies without paying a dime for software. Similar trading packages for equities and futures can cost over $1000. A worldwide community of traders and programmers has developed, offering hundreds of free and commercial expert advisors and indicators, as well as programming services and advice.

The similarity of MQL to languages such as C makes it relatively easy for experienced programmers to pick up, and the language itself is well documented. But learning how to effectively program trading strategies in MQL is a process of trial and error.

MQL is a relatively low level language, and as such, it is necessary for the programmer to create custom procedures to handle many common trading functions. Coding something as simple as a trailing stop, for example, can be daunting for the new MQL programmer.

There are many factors that must be taken into consideration when programming a robust automated trading strategy, and MetaTrader itself has many idiosyncrasies that the programmer needs to be aware of. It can take dozens of hours of troubleshooting and practice to learn the techniques necessary to program expert advisors.

This book hopes to shorten the learning curve for new expert advisor programmers. Here I will present many of the tips and tricks I've learned in the hundreds of hours I've spent coding expert advisors over the last few years.

About This Book

By the time you finish this book, you should possess the knowledge necessary to create your own robust automated trading strategies in MQL, including common trading features such as trailing stops, money management and much more. You will also learn how to construct a simple indicator, using built-in indicator functions.

This book assumes that the reader is knowledgeable about forex trading and technical analysis in general. The reader should already be proficient in using expert advisors and indicators in MetaTrader. While no prior programming knowledge is assumed, the reader will benefit from having some basic programming skills, and familiarity with concepts such as variables, control structures, functions and modern programming language syntax.

We will be diving right into coding solutions to specific problems. Every attempt is made to explain new concepts as they are introduced, however this book is not intended as a language reference. The MQL reference at **http://docs.mql4.com** does an excellent job at that. The MQL reference is also built into the MetaEditor IDE that comes with MetaTrader.

While we will attempt to touch on everything that is necessary and relevant to expert advisor development, we will not be able to cover every element of the MQL language. There are many specialized functions in MQL that are not generally used in expert advisor programing. In particular, we will not be discussing array functions, file manipulation, objects, windows, and most string or conversion functions.

The official MQL4 website at **http://www.mql4.com** has a free book on MQL programming that may serve as a useful and complementary resource. There are many informative articles that cover basic and advanced programming concepts in MQL, a code library with additional indicators and examples, and a forum where you can ask for help with your programming questions.

The code examples and techniques I teach in this book are what has worked for me. I try to keep things as simple as possible, without sacrificing functionality. That said, there is always more than one way to accomplish something, and this is especially true in programming. There are equally valid methods of achieving the same result, and it is possible you may discover a better way of doing something.

Many of the source code examples in this book, as well as the full appendixes, are available for download at the book's official website, **http://www.expertadvisorbook.com/**. This way, you can save yourself the time of typing in all of the examples yourself. Feel free to modify the source code for your own needs.

A Note About MQL 5

As of this writing, the next version of the MetaTrader platform is in open beta testing. There will be some significant changes to the newest version of MQL. MetaQuotes has reported that MetaTrader 5 will not be backward compatible with MetaTrader 4 programs. Thus, any programs written in MQL 4 will need to be rewritten or updated for MQL 5.

This book deals with MetaTrader 4, as it is the version I have been programming in for the last few years and is currently the version that is being used by Forex brokers. Since the release of MetaTrader 4 in 2005, Forex trading has exploded in popularity. MetaTrader has become the most popular forex trading platform, and there have been thousands of trading strategies and indicators written in MQL 4.

I predict the migration to MetaTrader 5 will be a gradual one. Brokers will continue to support MetaTrader 4 for some time, so the programs you write in MQL 4 will not become obsolete immediately. The concepts in this book will remain the same, although some of the functions and syntax will change. The challenge will be to learn the new MQL 5 features and incorporate it into your existing code.

A second edition of this book will be released sometime after the final release of MetaTrader 5. For those who have purchased this book, the updated source code and an MQL4 to MQL5 guide will be available at our website, `http://www.expertadvisorbook.com/`.

Conventions Used In This Book

MQL language elements, source code examples, and file and URL locations will be displayed in a `fixed-width font`. A larger bold font will be used for inline text. Blocks of source code will be indented. Any bold text appearing in an indented source code block indicates code that has been updated or changed from a previous example.

```
Source code block
Updated source code
```

Words in *italics* indicate a new concept that is being introduced or defined. References to sections and topics in the MQL Reference will be displayed in italics. References to elements of the MetaTrader 4 interface, including windows, dialogs, buttons or menu items, will also be displayed in italics.

Chapter 1
An Introduction to MQL

Introduction to MetaEditor

What is an Expert Advisor?

An *expert advisor* is an automated trading program written in MQL. Expert advisors (commonly abbreviated as EA) can place, modify and close orders according to a trading system algorithm. EA's generally use indicators to generate trading signals. These indicators can be the ones that come with MetaTrader, or they can be custom indicators.

An *indicator* is a technical analysis tool that calculates price data to give an interpretation of market activity. An indicator draws lines or objects on the chart. Indicators cannot place, modify or close orders. Examples of indicators include the moving average and stochastics.

A *script* is a simplified expert advisor that performs a single task, such as placing a pending order or closing all orders on a chart. A few useful scripts are included with MetaTrader.

File Formats

Files with the **.mq4** extension are *source code* files. These are the files we edit in MetaEditor. When an **.mq4** file is compiled, an **.ex4** file is produced.

Files with the **.ex4** extension are *executable* files. These are the files we run in MetaTrader. These files cannot be opened in MetaEditor. If you only have the **.ex4** file for an EA or indicator, the icon next to the file name in MetaTrader's *Navigator* window will be grayed out.

Files with the **.mqh** extension are *include* files. These files contain user-created functions that are referenced in an **.mq4** file. During compilation, the compiler "includes" the contents of the **.mqh** file in the **.ex4** file. We'll learn more about include files later.

The **.mqt** extension is used for template files. While these files can be opened in MetaTrader, the file type is not associated with the program in Windows. Templates are used to create new files using the Expert Advisor Wizard in MetaEditor.

You can create your own templates if you wish, but we will not be covering template creation in this book. The MetaTrader documentation will tell you all you need to know about creating templates.

Indicators, expert advisors, libraries and scripts all share the `.mq4` extension. The only way to tell them apart is either by their save location, or by opening the file and examining them. By the time you finish this book, you should be able to identify the difference between program types just by looking at the source code.

File Locations

All MetaEditor files are stored inside the *experts folder*. The `\experts` folder is contained in the MetaTrader installation directory, which is in `C:\Program Files\`. If your broker is Interbank FX, for example, the MT4 installation folder would be `C:\Program Files\Interbank FX Trader 4\`.

The `\experts` folder contains the source code and executable files for the expert advisors. Using the above example, the `\experts` folder would be located at `C:\Program Files\Interbank FX Trader 4\experts\`.

There are numerous folders inside the `\experts` folder that contain other types of source code and executable files. Here's a list of the save locations for all file types:

- `\experts\indicators` – Source code and executable files for your indicators are stored here.

- `\experts\include` – Source code include files with the `.mqh` extension are stored here.

- `\experts\libraries` – Function libraries and DLLs are stored here.

- `\experts\scripts` – Source code and executable files for scripts are stored here.

- `\experts\templates` – Templates for source code files are stored here.

There are a few other folders inside the experts folder that you'll want to be aware of too:

- `\experts\logs` – Activity logs for your expert advisors are stored here. These will be useful for debugging your expert advisors.

- `\experts\presets` – Expert advisor settings that are saved or loaded from MetaTrader's *Properties* dialog are stored here.

- `\experts\files` – Any files used for input or output must be stored here.

MetaEditor

MetaEditor is an Integrated Development Environment (IDE) for MQL that comes packaged with MetaTrader. It includes useful reference, search and auto-complete tools that makes coding in MQL a lot easier.

The *Editor* window allows you to have multiple files open at once. You can minimize, maximize and tab between several open windows. The *Navigator* window offers useful file-browsing and reference features. The *Toolbox* window displays help contents, compilation errors, file search results, and online access to articles and files at MQL4.com.

One of the most useful editing features is the Assistant. Simply type the first few characters of an MQL function, operator or other language element, and a drop-down list will appear. Press Enter to accept the highlighted suggestion and auto-complete the phrase.

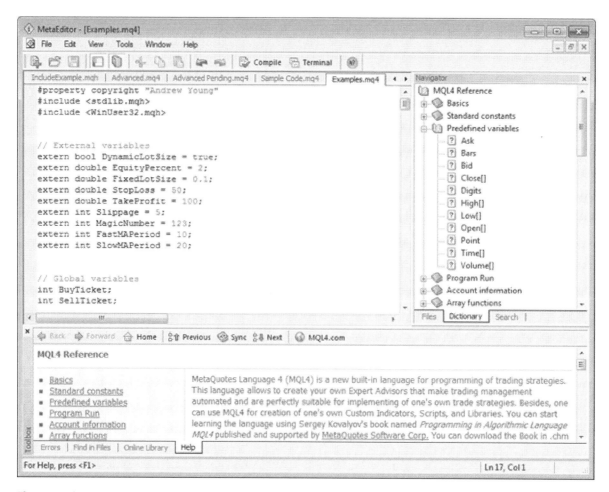

Fig. 1.1 – The MetaEditor interface. Clockwise from top left: Editor window, Navigator window, and Toolbox window.

The *Files* tab in the Navigator window is a simple file browser that allows you to open and edit any of the MQL files in your **\experts** folder. The *Dictionary* tab features a built-in MQL reference, while the *Search* tab is a search feature for the MQL reference.

The built-in MQL reference and the context-sensitive help will save you a lot of time when coding. If you need help remembering the syntax of a particular language element, select or place the text cursor on the element in the editor window. Press F1 on your keyboard and the help topic will appear in the Toolbox window.

```
// Open buy order
BuyTicket = OrderSen
    OrderLots
    OrderMagicNumber
    OrderModify
    OrderOpenPrice
    OrderOpenTime
    OrderPrint
    OrderProfit
    OrderSelect
    OrderSend
```

Fig. 1.2 – MetaEditor's Assistant auto complete feature.

The toolbar in MetaEditor features the standard complement of file and editing functions. The Navigator and Toolbox windows can be shown or hidden using their respective buttons on the toolbar.

The *Compile* button compiles the current file in the editor. If there are any compilation errors, they will be shown in the Toolbox window. The *Terminal* button opens the trading terminal for testing.

Basic Concepts

We're going to review some basic programming concepts that will make the rest of this book easier to understand for new programmers. If you're an experienced programmer, feel free to skip ahead to the next section, *Layout of an MQL File*.

Syntax

If you're familiar with programming in languages such as C++, PHP or one of the many languages whose syntax is derived from C, you'll be very comfortable programming in MQL. If your previous programming experience is in a language such as Visual Basic, then you may need to make a few adjustments.

In MQL, every statement is terminated with a semicolon. This is called an *expression.* An expression can span multiple lines, but there must be a semicolon at the end.

```
double LastHigh = High[1];

string MultiLine = StringConcatenate("This is a multi-line statement. ",
    "For clarity, we will indent multiple lines in this book");
```

If you're new to programing, or accustomed to programming in a language that does not terminate expressions with a semicolon, you'll need to make sure you're placing the semicolon at the end of every statement. Not terminating lines with a semicolon is a common newbie mistake.

There are a few exceptions to this: Compound operators do not need a semi-colon. A *compound operator* is a block of code that contains multiple expressions within braces {}. Examples of compound operators include control operators (**if, switch**), cycle operators (**for, while**) and function declarations.

```
if(Compound == true)
   {
      Print("This is a compound expression");
   }
```

Note that there is no semicolon after the initial **if** operator, nor is there a semicolon after the closing brace. There is a semicolon after the **Print()** function, however. There can be one, or multiple expressions inside the braces. Each must end with a semicolon.

Comments

Comments are useful for documenting your code, as well as for temporarily removing code while testing and debugging. You can comment out a single line with two forward slashes:

```
// This is a comment
```

A multi-line comment begins with /* and ends with */. A multi-line comment can span any number of lines, and everything between /* and */ is commented out.

```
/* This is a comment block
   Everything here is commented out */
```

Identifiers

Identifiers are names given to variables and custom functions. An identifier can be any combination of numbers, letters, and the underscore character (_). Identifiers can be up to 31 characters in length.

You'll want your identifiers to be descriptive of their function, but be sure your identifier doesn't match an MQL language element (also called a *reserved word*). Here's an example of a variable identifier and a custom function identifier. The identifier is in italics:

```
double StopLoss;
int Order_Count()
```

Identifiers in MQL are *case-sensitive.* This means that **StopLoss** and **stoploss** are different variables! This is another common newbie mistake, so check those identifier names!

Variables

A *variable* is the basic storage unit of any programming language. Variables hold data necessary for our program to function, such as prices, settings and indicator values.

Variables must be declared before they are used. To declare a variable, you specify it's *data type*, an identifier, and optionally a default value. If you declare a variable more than once, or not at all, you'll get a compilation error.

The *data type* specifies the type of information the variable holds, whether it be a number, a text string, a date or a color. Here are the data types in MQL:

- **int** – A integer (whole number) such as 0, 3, or -5. Any number assigned to an integer variable is rounded up to the next whole number.

- **double** – A fractional number such as 1.5765, 0.03 or -2.376. Use these for price data, or in mathematical expressions involving division.

- **string** – A text string such as **"The quick brown fox jumped over the lazy dog"**. Strings must be surrounded by double quotes.

- **boolean** – A **true**/**false** value. Can also be represented as 1 (true) or 0 (false). Use these anytime you need to evaluate an binary, or on/off condition.

- **datetime** – A time and date value such as **2009.01.01 00:00.** Internally, a datetime variable is represented as the number of seconds passed since January 1, 1970.

- **color** – A constant representing a color, such as **Red** or **DarkSlateBlue**. These are generally used for changing indicator or object colors.

Here's an example of a variable declaration. This is an integer variable, with the identifier **MyVariable** and a default value of 1.

```
int MyVariable = 1;
```

Once a variable has been declared, you can change its value by assigning a new value to it. Here's an example where we assign the number 5 to **MyVariable**:

```
MyVariable = 5;
```

You can also assign the value of one variable to another variable:

```
int YourVariable = 2;
MyVariable = YourVariable;
// MyVariable is 2
```

The assigned variable should be of the same data type. If a double is assigned to an integer variable, for example, the double will be rounded to the nearest whole number. This may lead to an undesirable result.

Constants

Just like its name suggests, a *constant* is a data value that never changes. For example, the number **5** is an integer constant, the letter **'A'** is a character constant, and **2009.01.01** is a datetime constant for January 1, 2009.

MQL has a wide variety of standard constants for things like price data, chart periods, colors and trade operations. For example **PERIOD_H1** is a constant for the H1 chart time frame, **OP_BUY** refers to a buy market order, and **Red** is a color constant for the color red.

You can even create your own constants using the **#define** preprocessor directive. We'll get to that shortly. You can learn more about MQL's standard constants in the *Standard Constants* section of the MQL Reference.

Functions

Functions are the building blocks of modern programming languages. A function is a block of code that is designed to carry out a certain task, such as placing an order or calculating a stop loss. MQL has dozens of built-in functions for everything from technical indicators to order placement.

Functions are designed to be reused over and over again. Learning how to create functions for common trading tasks is essential to productive programming. We will work on creating reusable functions for many of the tasks that we will learn in this book.

Let's start with a simple function called **PipPoint()**, that calculates the number of decimal points in the current pair, and automatically adjusts for 3 and 5 digit brokers so that the result is always equal to one pip. For Yen pairs (2 or 3 digits), the function returns 0.01. For all other pairs (4 and 5 digits), the function returns 0.0001. Here's how we would call the function from code:

```
double UsePoint;
UsePoint = PipPoint();
```

We declare a variable of type **double** named **UsePoint**. Then we call the **PipPoint()** function and assign the result to **UsePoint**. Now we can use the value stored in **UsePoint** to calculate a stop loss, for example.

Here is the code for the **PipPoint()** function:

```
double PipPoint()
  {
    if(Digits == 2 || Digits == 3) double UsePoint = 0.01;
    else if(Digits == 4 || Digits == 5) UsePoint = 0.0001;
    return(UsePoint);
  }
```

The first line is our function declaration. Like variables, function declarations have a data type and an identifier. Functions use the same data types as variables do. The data type is dependent on the type of data the function returns. Since this function returns a fractional number, we use the **double** data type.

The body of the function is contained within the brackets {}. We have an **if-else** statement that evaluates the number of digits after the decimal place, and assigns the appropriate value to the **UsePoint** variable. Following that, we have the **return** operator, which returns the value of **UsePoint** to the calling function.

There is a special data type for functions that do not return a value. The **void** data type is used for functions that carry out a specific task, but do not need to return a value to the calling function. **Void** functions do not require a **return** operator in the body of the function.

Let's consider a simple function for placing a buy order. This function has *arguments* that need to be passed to the function. This function will place a buy market order on the current symbol with the specified lot size, stop loss and take profit.

```
int OpenBuyOrder(double LotSize, double StopLoss, double TakeProfit)
  {
    int Ticket = OrderSend(Symbol(),OP_BUY,LotSize,Ask,StopLoss,TakeProfit);
    return(Ticket);
  }
```

This function has three arguments, **LotSize, StopLoss** and **TakeProfit**. Arguments are variables that are used only within the function. Their value is assigned by the calling function. Here's how we would call this function in code using constants:

```
OpenBuyOrder(2, 1.5550, 1.6050);
```

This will place a buy order of 2 lots, with a stop loss of 1.5550 and a take profit of 1.6050. Here's another example using variables. We'll assume that the variables **UseLotSize, BuyStopLoss** and **BuyTakeProfit** have the appropriate values assigned:

```
int GetTicket = OpenBuyOrder(UseLotSize,BuyStopLoss,BuyTakeProfit);
```

In this example, we are assigning the return value of **OpenBuyOrder()** to the variable **GetTicket**, which the ticket number of the order we just placed. Assigning the output of a function to a variable is optional. In this case, it is only necessary if you plan to do further processing using the ticket number of the placed order.

Arguments can have *default values*, which means that if a parameter is not explicitly passed to the function, the argument will take the default value. Default value arguments will always be at the end of the argument list. Here is an example of a function with several default values:

```
int DefaultValFunc(int Ticket, double Price, int Number = 0, string Comment = NULL)
```

This function has two arguments with default values, **Number** and **Comment**, with default values of **0** and **NULL** respectively. If we want to use the default values for both **Number** and **Comment**, we simply omit those arguments when calling the function:

```
DefaultValFunc(TicketNum,UsePrice);
```

Note that we only specified the first two arguments. **Number** and **Comment** use the default values of **0** and **NULL**. If we want to specify a value for **Number**, but not for **Comment**, we simply omit the last argument:

```
      DefaultValFunc(TicketNum,UsePrice,UseNumber);
```

Again, **Comment** uses the default value of **NULL**. But, if we want to specify a value for **Comment**, regardless of whether or not we want to use the default value for **Number**, we have to specify a value for **Number** as well:

```
      DefaultValFunc(TicketNum,UsePrice,0,"Comment String");
```

In this example, we used 0 as the value for **Number**, which is the same as the default value, and a string constant as the value for **Comment**. Remember that when you're dealing with multiple arguments that have default values, you can only omit arguments if you want to use the default values for all of the remaining arguments!

Variable Scope

The *scope* of a variable determines which functions it is available to, and how long it stays in memory. In MQL, scope can be *local* or *global*. A local variable can also be *static*.

A *local* variable is one that is declared inside a function. Local variables are only available inside the function it is declared in. The variable is initialized every time the function runs. Once the function exits, the variable and its data are cleared from memory.

An exception to this would be a *static* local variable. Static variables remain in memory even after the function exits. When the function is run again, the variable is not reinitialized, but instead retains it's previous value.

A static variable is declared by typing **static** in front of the variable declaration. Here's an example of a static variable declaration:

```
      static int MyStaticVar;
```

If a static variable needs to be made available to more than one function, use a global variable instead. In this case you do not need to declare the variable as static.

A *global* variable is one that is available to all functions inside a program. As long as the program is running, the value of the global variable is maintained. Global variables are declared outside of a function, generally at the top of the source code file.

There is no special method for initializing a global variable. The syntax is identical to that of a local variable.

Layout of an MQ4 File

Creating a New Expert Advisor

The *Expert Advisor Wizard* in MetaEditor is the quickest way to get started in creating an expert advisor. You can start the wizard by selecting *New* from the *File* menu, by pressing the *New* button on the toolbar, or by pressing *Ctrl+N* on your keyboard.

The dialog presents you with several options. You can create indicators, scripts, libraries and include files using the wizard. You can also choose a template for generating a file. The resulting file will be saved to the appropriate directory, depending on its type. Make sure *Expert Advisor* is chosen and press *Next*.

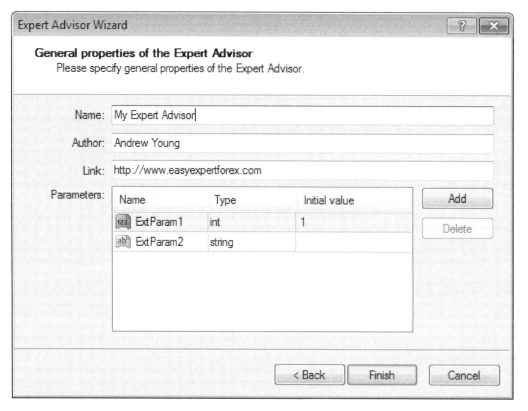

Fig. 1.3 – Expert Advisor Wizard general properties.

You will be prompted for a *Name*, *Author* and *Link*, as well as some optional parameters. The Name field will be the file name of your program. The EA will be saved to the `\experts` folder under that file name.

The contents of the Author field will appear next to the EA name in the Strategy Tester, and as a tooltip when you mouse over the EA name in the Navigator window. The Link field is a URL to your website, but it will not appear anywhere outside the source code file.

You can also enter your trade parameters here. For now, add a parameter or two, but don't bother adjusting them. It's best to simply add these manually to the source code later. Press the *Finish* button and an expert advisor template will open with your information already added.

The default expert advisor template is rather minimal, but it contains the basic structure of an expert advisor. Let's identify the layout of an MQL file using the expert advisor template as our guide.

Preprocessor Directives

The first thing to appear in any MQL file are the preprocessor directives. These are prefaced by a **#**. The default expert advisor template has two: **#property copyright**, which is the Author name you entered in the Expert Advisor Wizard, and **#property link**, which is the Link you entered in the wizard.

There are other **#property** directives, but almost all of them are related to indicators and scripts. The only **#property** directive you should include in your expert advisor is **#property copyright**, which identifies the EA as your creation.

A second type of preprocessor directive you will likely use is the **#include** directive. As mentioned earlier, an include file consists of functions and source code that will be included in your project when it is compiled. The syntax for the include directive is:

```
#include <filename.mqh>
```

The file **stdlib.mqh** in our example on page 19 is a standard include file that comes with MetaTrader. It includes several miscellaneous functions that programmers may find useful. Like all include files, it is located in the **\experts\include** folder.

The **#define** directive is used for declaring constants for use in our program. For example, instead of typing out a long text string every time you need to use it, you can define a constant and type that instead:

```
#define MYCONSTANT "This is a constant"
```

In this example, we can use the constant identifier **MYCONSTANT** in place of the text string in our code. The convention for constant identifiers is to use all capital letters. Although it is not absolutely necessary, for consistency's sake you should define all identifiers for constants using caps.

Sometimes, a function you'll need to use is already compiled in another file, such as another expert advisor, a library file (**.ex4**) or a Windows DLL file (**.dll**). You can import functions directly into a project using **#import** directives.

Libraries are similar to include files, but instead of including the source code in our project, we will execute the other file and call the function from it. We'll talk about using libraries later in the book.

Import directives are usually placed in include files, especially if there are many functions to import. But if you just need to import one or two functions, and an include file for them doesn't already exists, then go ahead and import them directly into your project.

For detailed examples of the **#import** directive, see the MQL Reference page *Importing of Functions*, and look at the include files in the **\experts\include** folder. Here is the syntax for the **#import** directive:

```
#import "library.ex4"
   double MyImportedFunction();
#import
```

In this example, the library file we are importing the function(s) from is **library.ex4**. We are importing a single function of type double, called **MyImportedFunction()**. The function identifier must match the function name in the source library file. Note the semicolon at the end of the function declaration.

Parameters and External Variables

The next section in our expert advisor source code file are the external variables. These are the adjustable parameters for our trading system. This includes your trade settings (stop loss, take profit, lot size) and indicator settings. When you open the *Expert Properties* dialog for an expert advisor, you are viewing the external variables for that program.

We specify an external variable by adding **extern** in front of the variable. This specifies that the variable will appear in the Expert Properties dialog, and will be viewable and adjustable by the user.

```
extern double StopLoss = 50;
```

Be sure that the identifier for your external variable is descriptive of what it actually does. ("StopLoss" is better than "stop" or "SL", for example). You have 31 characters to describe your variable, so make the most of it. The default value for your variable will also be the default for that parameter, so choose a logical default value.

Global Variables

We declare any global variables at the top of our source code file, generally after the external variables. The location does not matter, as long as both the global and external variables are placed outside of and before any functions.

A global variable is one that is available to any function in the program. As long as the program is running, the global variable and it's value stays in memory, and can be referenced and changed by any function in the program.

Technically, external variables are global as well, but the global variables we're discussing in this section are internal, which means they are not viewable or changeable by the user.

Special Functions

MQL has 3 built-in functions to control program execution: `init()`, `deinit()` and `start()`. The `init()` function is comprised of code that is run once, when the EA is first started. The `init()` function is optional, and can be left out if you're not using it.

The `deinit()` function consists of code that is run once, when the EA is stopped. This function is also optional, and it's unlikely you will need to use it in an expert advisor.

The `start()` function contains the main program code, and is required in your EA. Every time the start function is run, your trading conditions are checked, and orders are placed or closed depending on how those conditions are evaluated.

The `start()` function is run on every tick. A *tick* is a price movement, or change in the Bid or Ask price for a currency pair. During active markets, there may be several ticks per second. During slow markets, minutes can pass by without a tick.

Other Functions

Any other functions that your EA may use should be declared after the **start()** function. These functions will be called from the **start()**, **init()** or **deinit()** functions, or from other functions that are called from the main program. We'll cover custom functions later in the book.

```
// Preprocessor Directives
#property copyright "Andrew Young"
#property link       "http://www.expertadvisorbook.com"

#include <stdlib.mqh>

#define MYCONSTANT "This is a constant"


// External Parameters
extern int Parameter1 = 1;
extern double Parameter2 = 0.01;


// Global Variables
int GlobalVariable1;


// Init function
int init()
  {
    // Startup code
    return(0);
  }


// Deinit function
int deinit()
  {
    // Shutdown code
    return(0);
  }


// Start function
int start()
  {
    // Main code
    return(0);
  }


// Custom functions
int MyCustomFunction()
  {
    // Custom code
    return(0);
  }
```

Fig 1.4 – Sample expert advisor layout

Chapter 2
Order Placement

Bid, Ask & Spread

As a Forex trader, you're probably already familiar with the Bid and Ask prices. But you might not be aware of their role in order placement. It is very important to use the correct price when opening or closing orders.

The *Bid* price is what you see on the MetaTrader charts. It is usually what we think of when we think of the "current price." The *Ask* price is generally just a few pips above the Bid price. The difference between the Bid and the Ask is the the *spread*, which is the broker's commission for placing the order.

The Ask price is where we <u>open buy orders</u>, and <u>close sell orders</u>. The Bid price is where we <u>open sell orders</u>, and <u>close buy orders</u>. You'll need to indicate the correct price when opening a market order, or when closing an order at market, so remember the difference between the two.

Order Types

There are three types of orders that can be placed in MetaTrader: market, stop and limit orders. Market orders are the most common. A *market order* opens a position immediately at the prevailing Bid or Ask price.

When placing a market order in MQL, we must specify an opening price (generally the latest Bid or Ask quote). If the specified opening price is outdated, due to a fast moving market or a delay in program execution, the terminal will attempt to place the order at the current market price, provided it is within the maximum *slippage*.

If you place a market order using the *New Order* dialog in MetaTrader, you'll see a setting at the bottom labeled "Enable maximum deviation from quoted price." When this is checked, you can then specify the maximum deviation in pips. This is the maximum slippage.

If the current price falls outside of our specified opening price, plus or minus the slippage, a requote error will occur and the order will not be placed. You may have noticed this when attempting to place a market order during a fast moving market. Note that ECN/STP brokers do not use a slippage setting, and will always open market orders at the current price.

A *stop* order is a type of pending order. *Pending* orders are a request to open a market order at a certain price. A *buy stop* order is placed <u>above</u> the current price, while a *sell stop* order is placed <u>below</u> the current price. The expectation is that the price will eventually rise or fall to that level and continue in that direction, resulting in a profit.

A *limit* order is the opposite of a stop order. A *buy limit* order is placed <u>below</u> the current price, while a *sell limit* order is placed <u>above</u> the current price. The expectation is that the price will rise or fall to that level, triggering the order, and then reversing. Limit orders are not used very often in automated trading.

An *expiration* time can be set for pending orders. If the order is not filled by the expiration time, the order is automatically deleted. Not all brokers support trade expiration.

The Order Placement Process

The process of placing an order in MQL involves several steps. We must determine the following before placing the order:

- The type of order to be placed – buy or sell; stop, market or limit.

- The currency pair to trade – generally the chart that the EA is attached to.

- The lot size. This can either be a fixed lot size, or one that is calculated using a money management routine.

- The order opening price. For market orders, this will be the current Bid or Ask price. For pending orders, the opening price must be a minimum distance from the current price, and should be above or below the current price as required by the order type.

- The stop loss price. The stop loss can be a predetermined price, an indicator value, a fixed number of pips from the order opening price, or it can be dynamically calculated using a risk management routine. The stop loss can be placed with the order, or it can be added to the order afterward.

- The take profit price. This is generally a fixed number of pips from the order opening price, although it can be calculated using other methods as well. The take profit can be placed with the order, or it can be added to the order afterward.

- Order identifiers such as an order comment, or a "magic number" that identifies an order as being placed by a specific expert advisor.

- An optional expiration price for pending orders, if the broker supports it.

OrderSend()

The `OrderSend()` function is used to place orders in MQL. The syntax is as follows:

```
int OrderSend(string Symbol, int Type, double Lots, double Price,
   int Slippage, double StopLoss, double TakeProfit, string Comment = NULL,
   int MagicNumber = 0, datetime Expiration = 0, color Arrow = CLR_NONE);
```

- **Symbol** – A string representing the currency pair to trade, for example **GBPUSD**. The `Symbol()` function is used for the current chart's currency pair.

- **Type** – The type of order to place: buy or sell; market, stop or limit. This is an integer value, represented by the following constants:

  - **OP_BUY** – Buy market order (integer value 0).

  - **OP_SELL** – Sell market order (integer value 1).

  - **OP_BUYSTOP** – Buy stop order (integer value 2).

  - **OP_SELLSTOP** – Sell stop order (integer value 3).

  - **OP_BUYLIMIT** – Buy limit order (integer value 4).

  - **OP_SELLLIMIT** – Sell limit order (integer value 5).

- **Lots** – The number of lots to trade. You can specify mini lots (0.1) or micro lots (0.01) if your broker supports it.

- **Price** – The price at which to open the order. For a buy market order, this will be the **Ask**. For a sell market order, this will be the **Bid**. For pending orders, this will be any valid price that is above or below the current price.

- **Slippage** – The maximum slippage in points. Use a sufficiently large setting when auto trading. Brokers that do not use slippage will ignore this parameter.

- **StopLoss** – The stop loss price. For a buy order, the stop loss price is below the order opening price, and for a sell order, above. If set to 0, no stop loss will be used.

- **TakeProfit** – The take profit price. For a buy order, the take profit is above the order opening price, and for a sell order, below. If set to 0, no take profit will be used.

- **Comment** – An optional string that will serve as an order comment. Comments are shown under the *Trade* tab in the *Terminal* window. Order comments can also be used as an order identifier.

- **MagicNumber** – An optional integer value that will identify the order as being placed by a specific expert advisor. It is highly recommended that you use this.

- **Expiration** – An optional expiration time for pending orders. Not all brokers accept trade expiration times – for these brokers, an error will result if an expiration time is specified.

- **Arrow** – An optional color for the arrow that will be drawn on the chart, indicating the opening price and time. If no color is specified, the arrow will not be drawn.

The `OrderSend()` function returns the ticket number of the order that was just placed. If no order was placed, due to an error condition, the return value will be **-1**.

We can save the order ticket to a global or static variable for later use. If the order was not placed due to an error condition, we can analyze the error and take appropriate action based on the returned error code.

Placing A Market Order

Here's an example of a buy market order. We'll assume that the variables `LotSize`, `Slippage`, `BuyStopLoss`, `BuyTakeProfit` and `MagicNumber` have already been calculated or assigned and are valid.

```
OrderSend(Symbol(),OP_BUY,LotSize,Ask,Slippage,BuyStopLoss,BuyTakeProfit,
    "Buy Order",MagicNumber,0,Green);
```

The `Symbol()` function returns the current chart symbol. We will be placing orders on the current chart pair 99% of the time. `OP_BUY` indicates that this is a buy market order. `Ask` is a predefined variable in MQL that stores the most recent Ask quote. (Remember that buy orders open at the Ask price!)

The `Slippage` is set using an external variable. The slippage parameter is an integer, indicating the number of points to allow for price slippage. If your broker uses 4 digit quotes (2 for Yen pairs), 1 point would be equal to 1 pip. If your broker offers 3 and 5 digit quotes however, then 1 point would be 0.1 pips. In this case, you'd need to add an additional zero to the end of your `Slippage` setting.

We've added the generic comment **"Buy Order"** to this order. Since there is no expiration for market orders, the Expiration parameter is 0. Finally, we specify the color constant `Green` to draw a green arrow on the chart.

Here is an example of a sell market order, using the same parameters as above:

```
OrderSend(Symbol(),OP_SELL,LotSize,Bid,Slippage,SellStopLoss,SellTakeProfit,
   "Sell Order",MagicNumber,0,Red);
```

We use **OP_SELL** as the order type, to specify a sell market order. We use **Bid** as the order opening price, to reflect the fact that sell orders open at the Bid price. **"Sell Order"** is our order comment, and we use **Red** as the arrow color to differentiate from buy orders.

Placing a Pending Stop Order

The difference between pending orders and market orders is that the order opening price will be something other than the current market price. The stop loss and take profit values must be calculated relative to the pending order opening price.

In these examples, we will use the variable **PendingPrice** for our pending order price. It can be calculated based on our trading algorithm, or it can be set as an external parameter.

For a buy stop order, **PendingPrice** must be greater than the current Ask price. We'll assume that **BuyStopLoss** and **BuyTakeProfit** have been correctly calculated relative to **PendingPrice**. Here's an example of a buy stop order placement:

```
OrderSend(Symbol(),OP_BUYSTOP,LotSize,PendingPrice,Slippage,BuyStopLoss,
   BuyTakeProfit,"Buy Stop Order",MagicNumber,0,Green);
```

Note that we use **OP_BUYSTOP** to indicate a buy stop order, and **PendingPrice** for our order opening price. No expiration time has been indicated for this order.

For a sell stop order, **PendingPrice** must be less than the current Bid price. In this example, we'll add an order expiration time, using the variable **Expiration**. The expiration time must be greater than the current server time. Here's an example of a sell stop order placement:

```
OrderSend(Symbol(),OP_SELLSTOP,LotSize,PendingPrice,Slippage,SellStopLoss,
   SellTakeProfit,"Sell Stop Order",MagicNumber,Expiration,Red);
```

Placing a Pending Limit Order

Limit orders are similar to stop orders, except that the pending order price is reversed, relative to the current price and the order type. For buy limit orders, the pending order price must be less than the current Bid price. Here's an example of a buy limit order:

```
OrderSend(Symbol(),OP_BUYLIMIT,LotSize,PendingPrice,Slippage,BuyStopLoss,
    BuyTakeProfit,"Buy Limit Order",MagicNumber,0,Green);
```

Note that we used **OP_BUYLIMIT** to indicate a buy limit order. Otherwise, our parameters are identical to those for stop orders.

For a sell limit order, the pending order price must be greater than the current Ask price. Here's an example of a sell limit order:

```
OrderSend(Symbol(),OP_SELLLIMIT,LotSize,PendingPrice,Slippage,SellStopLoss,
    SellTakeProfit,"Sell Limit Order",MagicNumber,Expiration,Red);
```

Calculating Stop Loss & Take Profit

There are several ways of calculating stop loss and take profit prices. The most common method is to specify the number of pips away from the order opening price to place your stop. For example, if we have a stop loss setting of 50 pips, that means that the stop loss price will be 50 pips away from our order opening price.

We can also use an indicator value, an external parameter or some other type of price calculation. All we will need to do then is verify that the stop loss or take profit price is valid.

Calculating in Pips

For this, the most common method of calculating stops, we will use an external variable in which the user specifies the number of pips for the stop loss and take profit. We then calculate the stops relative to the order opening price.

For buy market orders, the opening price will be the **Ask**, and for sell market orders, the opening price will be the **Bid**. For pending stop and limit orders, we assign a a valid opening price that is something other than the current market price. We will assign the appropriate price to the variable **OpenPrice**.

Here are the external variables we'll use for our stop loss and take profit settings:

```
extern int StopLoss = 50;
extern int TakeProfit = 100;
```

In this example, we've entered a stop loss of 50 pips, and a take profit of 100 pips. You've likely seen settings similar to these in the EAs you've used.

To calculate our stop loss, we need to add or subtract 50 pips from our order opening price. First, we need to convert the integer value of 50 to the fractional value we'll use to add or subtract from the opening price. For Yen pairs, 50 pips is equal to 0.50. For all other pairs, it's 0.0050.

To convert an integer to the appropriate fractional value, we need to multiply our external **StopLoss** variable by the *Point*.

Point

Point is a predefined variable in MQL that returns the smallest price unit of a currency, depending on the number of decimal places. For a 4 decimal place currency pair, the point is 0.0001. For a Yen pair, it's 0.01.

Let's calculate the stop loss for a buy market order. We'll assign the current Ask price to **OpenPrice**, and use that as our order opening price. We'll check to see if our **StopLoss** setting is greater than zero. If so, we'll multiply the **StopLoss** by the **Point**. Then we'll subtract that from **OpenPrice**. The result will be stored in the variable **BuyStopLoss**.

```
double OpenPrice = Ask;

if(StopLoss > 0) double BuyStopLoss = OpenPrice - (StopLoss * Point);
// 1.4600 - (50 * 0.0001) = 1.4550
```

If **StopLoss** is not greater than zero, then **BuyStopLoss** is initialized with a value of 0, and no stop loss will be placed with the order. Assuming that **Point** is equal to 0.0001, if the order opening price is 1.4600, and our stop loss is 50 pips, then the stop loss price for the buy order will be 1.4600 - (0.0050) = 1.4550.

Recently, many brokers have been moving towards fractional pip price quotes, with 3 decimal places for Yen pairs and 5 decimal places for all other pairs. If our broker uses fractional pip quotes, then in our example above, **Point** would be equal to 0.00001.

If we use a point value of 0.00001 in our stop loss calculation example above, the stop loss would be calculated as 5 pips from the opening price, instead of 50 pips. This poses a problem. To get the correct value, we would have to add an extra zero to our stop loss setting – *i.e.* **StopLoss** = 500.

Instead of requiring the user to add an additional zero to their stop loss and take profit settings every time they trade on a fraction pip broker, we'll create a function that will always return 0.01 or 0.0001, regardless of whether or not the broker uses fractional pips. We'll call this function **PipPoint**, because it will always return the point value that is equal to one pip.

```
double PipPoint(string Currency)
   {
      int CalcDigits = MarketInfo(Currency,MODE_DIGITS);
      if(CalcDigits == 2 || CalcDigits == 3) double CalcPoint = 0.01;
      else if(CalcDigits == 4 || CalcDigits == 5) CalcPoint = 0.0001;
      return(CalcPoint);
   }
```

The string argument **Currency** is the symbol of the currency pair that we want to retrieve the point for. The **MarketInfo()** function with the **MODE_DIGITS** parameter returns the number of decimal places (digits) for that pair. The **if-else** statement assigns the appropriate point value to the **CalcPoint** variable, depending on the number of digits.

Here's an example of the usage of this function. You will be using the current chart pair the vast majority of the time, so we will pass the **Symbol()** function as the argument. This will return the point for the current chart.

```
double UsePoint = PipPoint(Symbol());
```

Here's a set of examples using specific pairs:

```
double UsePoint = PipPoint(EURUSD);
// Result is 0.0001

double UsePoint = PipPoint(USDJPY);
// Result is 0.01
```

We will be using this function to find the single pip point value for the remainder of this book. As we've demonstrated, the **Point** variable won't work correctly on fractional pip brokers when calculating the value of a single pip. You can never assume that the EA will only be used on a 2 and 4 digit broker, so it is necessary to automatically determine the point value of a single pip using **PipPoint()**.

Slippage and Point

Let's digress for a minute and create a function to resize the slippage parameter properly. As mentioned earlier in this chapter, on a broker with fractional pip quotes, the slippage parameter for the **OrderSend()** function will need to be increased by a factor of 10 to get the correct slippage value.

This function will automatically set the slippage parameter to the number of pips specified by the external **Slippage** parameter:

```
int GetSlippage(string Currency, int SlippagePips)
  {
    int CalcDigits = MarketInfo(Currency,MODE_DIGITS);
    if(CalcDigits == 2 || CalcDigits == 4) double CalcSlippage = SlippagePips;
    else if(CalcDigits == 3 || CalcDigits == 5) CalcSlippage = SlippagePips * 10;
    return(CalcSlippage);
  }
```

We pass the currency symbol and the external slippage parameter as arguments. If the currency uses 2 or 4 digit quotes, we use the unchanged **SlippagePips** argument as our slippage setting. If the currency uses 3 or 5 digit quotes, we multiply **SlippagePips** by 10. Here is how we use this function in **OrderSend()**:

```
// External parameters
extern int Slippage = 5;

// Order placement
OrderSend(Symbol(),OP_BUY,LotSize,Ask,GetSlippage(Symbol(),Slippage),BuyStopLoss,
  BuyTakeProfit,"Buy Order",MagicNumber,0,Green);
```

The slippage in this example will be 5 pips, and the slippage parameter will be automatically adjusted based on the number of digits in the currency quote.

Slippage and Point as Global Variables

The disadvantage of using a function to return the point or slippage value is the extra typing required for the function arguments. We'll create global variables that will hold the appropriate point and slippage values for our currency pair, and we'll use those anytime we need to reference those values.

Since these values will never change during program execution, we'll calculate these values in the **init()** function. We'll assume that the external integer variable **Slippage** is already present:

```
// Global variables
double UsePoint;
int UseSlippage;

int init()
  {
    UsePoint = PipPoint(Symbol());
    UseSlippage = GetSlippage(Symbol(),Slippage);
  }
```

From now on, we'll use **UsePoint** and **UseSlippage** to refer to these values. The above code assumes that your EA is placing orders on one currency only. This will be the case 98% of the time, but if you're creating an expert advisor that places orders on multiple currencies (or on a currency other than the current chart), you'll need to use the **PipPoint()** and **GetSlippage()** functions every time you need to calculate these values.

MarketInfo()

We used the **MarketInfo()** function above to retrieve the Point value and the number of digits in the currency quote. The **MarketInfo()** function has many uses, and you will be using it to retrieve necessary price information in your programs. Here is the syntax for the **MarketInfo()** function:

```
double MarketInfo(string Symbol, int RequestType);
```

The **Symbol** argument is simply the currency symbol that you want to retrieving the information for. For the current chart symbol, the **Symbol()** function can be used. For other symbols, you'll need to specify the currency symbol, such as **EURJPY**.

RequestType is an integer constant, representing the information that you are requesting from the function. Here's a list of the most useful **MarketInfo()** constants. A complete list can be found in the MQL Reference, under *Standard Constants – MarketInfo*.

- **MODE_POINT** – The point value. For example, 0.01 or 0.00001.

- **MODE_DIGITS** – The number of decimal places in the price. Will be 2 or 3 for Yen pairs, and 4 or 5 for all other pairs.

- **MODE_SPREAD** – The current spread. For example, 3 pips (or 30 for a fractional pip broker).

- **MODE_STOPLEVEL** – The stop level. For example, 3 pips (or 30 for a fractional pip broker).

These request identifiers are generally used when checking price information on another currency, or anywhere where the symbol may be anything other than the current chart symbol:

- **MODE_BID** – The current bid price of the selected symbol.

- **MODE_ASK** – The current ask price of the selected symbol.

- **MODE_LOW** – The low of the current bar of the selected symbol.

- **MODE_HIGH** – The high of the current bar of the selected symbol.

Calculating the Stop Loss

Now that we've determined the proper point value, it's time to calculate our stop loss. For buy orders, the stop loss will be below the order opening price, and for sell orders, the stop loss will be above the order opening price.

Here's our buy order stop loss calculation from earlier, with the **UsePoint** variable added. Note that we've assigned the **Ask** price to the **OpenPrice** variable:

```
double OpenPrice = Ask;
if(StopLoss > 0) double BuyStopLoss = OpenPrice - (StopLoss * UsePoint);
```

And here's the calculation for a sell order. Note that we've assigned the **Bid** price to **OpenPrice**, and that we are simply adding instead of subtracting:

```
double OpenPrice = Bid;
if(StopLoss > 0) double SellStopLoss = OpenPrice + (StopLoss * UsePoint);
```

For pending orders, the stop loss will be calculated relative to the pending order price. In this case, use the variable **OpenPrice** to store the pending order price instead of the current market price. The logic will be identical to the examples above.

Calculating the Take Profit

Calculating the take profit price is similar to calculating the stop loss, except we'll be reversing addition and subtraction. For a buy order, the take profit price will be above the order opening price, and for a sell order, the take profit price will be below the order opening price. We'll assume that the appropriate price has been assigned to **OpenPrice**:

```
if(TakeProfit > 0) double BuyTakeProfit = OpenPrice + (TakeProfit * UsePoint);

if(TakeProfit > 0) double SellTakeProfit = OpenPrice - (TakeProfit * UsePoint);
```

Alternate Stop Loss Methods

There are other ways of determining stop loss and take profit prices. For example, a recent high or low, or an indicator value could be used to determine a stop loss. Let's demonstrate how we could calculate these.

Let's say we're using a trading system that places the stop loss 2 pips below the low of the current bar. We use the predefined price array `Low[]` to retrieve the low of a bar. `Low[0]` is the low of the current bar, `Low[1]` is the low of the previous bar, and so on.

Once we've determined the low of the current bar, we multiply 2 by `UsePoint` to get a decimal value, and subtract that from our low:

```
double BuyStopLoss = Low[0] - (2 * UsePoint);
```

So if the low of the bar is 1.4760, the stop loss will be placed at 1.4758.

But maybe you want to place your stop loss at the lowest low of the last *x* number of bars. There's a function built into MetaTrader just for that. `iLowest()` returns the shift value indicating the bar with the lowest value in a specified time range. We can use high, low, open or close values.

Here's an example of how we would use `iLowest()` to find the lowest low of the last 10 bars:

```
int CountBars = 10;
int LowestShift = iLowest(NULL,0,MODE_LOW,CountBars,0);
double BuyStopLoss = Low[LowestShift];
```

The first parameter of `iLowest()` is the currency symbol – `NULL` means that we're using the current symbol. Many functions in MQL use the string constant `NULL` to refer to the current chart symbol. The second parameter is the chart period – `0` refers to the current chart frame.

`MODE_LOW` is an integer constant that specifies the low price series array. In other words, we're looking for the lowest low of the last `CountBars`. If we wanted to find the lowest close, for example, we would use `MODE_CLOSE`. You can find all of the series array constants in the MQL Reference under *Standard Constants – Series Arrays*.

`CountBars` is the number of bars we want to search, in this case 10. Finally, the last parameter is our starting location. 0 is the current bar. To start at a previous bar, count backward from the current bar – the previous bar is 1, the bar before that is 2, etc.

The output of the `iLowest()` function is an integer indicating the backward shift of the bar with the lowest value in the price series. In the example above, if `iLowest()` returns a 6, that means that the lowest low is 6 bars back. We store that value in the variable `LowestShift`. To find the actual price, we simply retrieve the price value of `Low[LowestShift]`, or in other words, `Low[6]`.

If you wanted to calculate a stop loss for a sell order using this method, the **iHighest()** function works the same way. Referencing the example above, you would use **MODE_HIGH** for your series array parameter.

Here's an example using an indicator. Let's say we have a moving average, and we want to use the moving average line as our stop loss. We'll use the variable **MA** to represent the moving average value for the current bar. All you need to do is assign the current moving average value to the stop loss:

```
double BuyStopLoss = MA;
```

If the moving average line is currently at 1.6894, then that will be our stop loss.

These are simply the most common methods of determining a stop loss or take profit price. Other methods can be developed using your knowledge of technical analysis or your imagination.

Retrieving Order Information

Once we've successfully placed an order, we'll need to retrieve some information about the order if we want to modify or close it. We do this using the **OrderSelect()** function. To use **OrderSelect()**, we can either use the ticket number of the order, or we can loop through the pool of open orders and select each of them in order.

Once we've selected an order using **OrderSelect()**, we can use a variety of order information functions to return information about the order, including the current stop loss, take profit, order opening price, closing price and more.

OrderSelect()

Here is the syntax for the **OrderSelect**() function:

```
bool OrderSelect(int Index, int Select, int Pool = MODE_TRADES)
```

- **Index** – This is either the ticket number of the order that we want to select, or the position in the order pool. The **Select** parameter will indicate which of these we are using.

- **Select** – A constant indicating whether the **Index** parameter is a ticket number or an order pool position:

  ○ **SELECT_BY_TICKET** – The value of the **Index** parameter is an order ticket number.

  ○ **SELECT_BY_POS** – The value of the **Index** parameter is an order pool position.

- **Pool** – An optional constant indicating the order pool: pending/open orders, or closed orders.

  - ○ **MODE_TRADES** – By default, we are examining the pool of currently opened orders.

  - ○ **MODE_HISTORY** – Examines the closed order pool (the order history).

If the **OrderSelect()** function locates the order successfully, the return value will be **true**, otherwise, the return value will be **false**.

Here's an example of the **OrderSelect**() function using an order ticket number. The **Ticket** variable should contain a valid order ticket:

```
OrderSelect(Ticket,SELECT_BY_TICKET);
```

After the **OrderSelect**() function has been called, we can use any of the order information functions to retrieve information about that order. A complete listing of functions that can be used with **OrderSelect**() can be found in the MQL Reference under *Trading Functions*. Here's a list of the most commonly used order information functions:

- **OrderSymbol()** – The symbol of the instrument that the selected order was placed on.

- **OrderType()** - The order type of the selected order: buy or sell; market, stop or limit. The return value is an integer corresponding to the order type constants on page 22.

- **OrderOpenPrice()** – The opening price of the selected order.

- **OrderLots()** – The lot size of the selected order.

- **OrderStopLoss()** – The stop loss price of the selected order.

- **OrderTakeProfit()** – The take profit price of the selected order.

- **OrderTicket()** – The ticket number of the selected order. Generally used when cycling through the order pool with the **SELECT_BY_POS** parameter.

- **OrderMagicNumber()** – The magic number of the selected order. When cycling through orders, you'll need to use this to identify orders placed by your EA.

- **OrderComment()** – The comment that was placed with the order. This can be used as a secondary order identifier.

- **OrderClosePrice()** – The closing price of the selected order. The order must already be closed (*i.e.* present in the order history pool).

- **OrderOpenTime()** – The opening time of the selected order.

- **OrderCloseTime()** – The closing time of the selected order.

- **OrderProfit()** – Returns the profit (in the deposit currency) for the selected order.

We'll need to use **OrderSelect()** before closing or modifying an order. Let's illustrate how we use **OrderSelect()** to close an order.

Closing Orders

When we close a market order, we are exiting the trade at the current market price. For buy orders, we close at the Bid price, and for sell orders, we close at the Ask. For pending orders, we simply delete the order from the trade pool.

OrderClose()

We close market orders using the **OrderClose()** function. Here is the syntax:

```
bool OrderClose(int Ticket, double Lots, double Price, int Slippage, color Arrow);
```

- **Ticket** – The ticket number of the market order to close.

- **Lots** – The number of lots to close. Most brokers allow partial closes.

- **Price** – The preferred price at which to close the trade. For buy orders, this will be the current Bid price, and for sell orders, the current Ask price.

- **Slippage** – The allowed slippage from the closing price, in pips.

- **Color** – A color constant for the closing arrow. If no color is indicated, no arrow will be drawn.

You can close part of a trade by specifying a partial lot size. For example, if you have a trade open with a lot size of 2.00, and you want to close half of the trade, then specify 1 lot for the **Lots** argument. Note that not all brokers support partial closes.

It is recommended that if you need to close a position in several parts, you should place multiple orders instead of doing partial closes. Using the example above, you would place two orders of 1.00 lot each, then simply close one of the orders when you want to close out half of the position. In this book, we will always be closing out the full order.

The following example closes a buy market order:

```
OrderSelect(CloseTicket,SELECT_BY_TICKET);
```

```
if(OrderCloseTime() == 0 && OrderType() == OP_BUY)
  {
    double CloseLots = OrderLots();
    double ClosePrice = Bid;

    bool Closed = OrderClose(CloseTicket,CloseLots,ClosePrice,UseSlippage,Red);
  }
```

The **CloseTicket** variable is the ticket number of the order we wish to close. The **OrderSelect()** function selects the order, and allows us to retrieve the order information. We use **OrderCloseTime()** to check the order closing time to see if the order has already been closed. If **OrderCloseTime()** returns 0, then we know the order has not been closed yet.

We also need to check the order type, since the order type determines the closing price for the order. The **OrderType()** function returns an integer indicating the order type. If it's a buy market order, indicated by **OP_BUY**, we'll continue closing the order.

Next, we retrieve the order lot size using **OrderLots()**, and store that value in **CloseLots**. We assign the current **Bid** price to **ClosePrice**. Then we call the **OrderClose()** function to close out our order.

We specify our Slippage setting with **UseSlippage**, and indicate a **Red** arrow to be printed on the chart. A boolean return value is stored in the variable **Closed**. If the order has been closed successfully, the value of **Closed** will be **true**, otherwise **false**.

To close a sell market order, all you need to do is change the order type to **OP_SELL** and assign the current **Ask** price to **ClosePrice**:

```
if(OrderCloseTime() == 0 && OrderType() == OP_SELL)
  {
    double CloseLots = OrderLots();
    double ClosePrice = Ask;

    bool Closed = OrderClose(CloseTicket,CloseLots,ClosePrice,UseSlippage,Red);
  }
```

OrderDelete()

There is a separate function for closing pending orders. **OrderDelete()** has two arguments, the ticket number and the arrow color. No closing price, lot size or slippage is required. Here is the code to close a pending buy stop order:

```
OrderSelect(CloseTicket,SELECT_BY_TICKET);

if(OrderCloseTime() == 0 && OrderType() == OP_BUYSTOP)
  {
    bool Deleted = OrderDelete(CloseTicket,Red);
  }
```

As we did with the `OrderClose()` function above, we need to check the order type to be sure it is a pending order. The pending order type constants are `OP_BUYSTOP`, `OP_SELLSTOP`, `OP_BUYLIMIT` and `OP_SELLLIMIT`. To close other types of pending orders, simply change the order type.

If the order has been filled, then it is now a market order, and must be closed using `OrderClose()` instead.

A Simple Expert Advisor

Let's see how the code we've discussed so far would work in an expert advisor. This is a simple moving average cross system. A buy order is opened when the 10 period moving average is greater than the 20 period moving average. When the 10 period moving average is less than the 20 period moving average, a sell order is opened.

This EA will alternate between opening buy and sell orders. Orders will be closed when an order is opened in the opposite direction, or by stop loss or take profit. We will use the global variables `BuyTicket` and `SellTicket` to store the last order ticket. When a new order is opened, the last order ticket is cleared. This prevents multiple consecutive orders from opening.

```
#property copyright "Andrew Young"


// External variables
extern double LotSize = 0.1;
extern double StopLoss = 50;
extern double TakeProfit = 100;

extern int Slippage = 5;
extern int MagicNumber = 123;

extern int FastMAPeriod = 10;
extern int SlowMAPeriod = 20;


// Global variables
int BuyTicket;
int SellTicket;
```

```
double UsePoint;
int UseSlippage;


// Init function
int init()
  {
    UsePoint = PipPoint(Symbol());
    UseSlippage = GetSlippage(Symbol(),Slippage);
  }


// Start function
int start()
  {
    // Moving averages
    double FastMA = iMA(NULL,0,FastMAPeriod,0,0,0,0);
    double SlowMA = iMA(NULL,0,SlowMAPeriod,0,0,0,0);

    // Buy order
    if(FastMA > SlowMA && BuyTicket == 0)
      {
        OrderSelect(SellTicket,SELECT_BY_TICKET);

        // Close order
        if(OrderCloseTime() == 0 && SellTicket > 0)
          {
            double CloseLots = OrderLots();
            double ClosePrice = Ask;

            bool Closed = OrderClose(SellTicket,CloseLots,ClosePrice,UseSlippage,Red);
          }

        double OpenPrice = Ask;

        // Calculate stop loss and take profit
        if(StopLoss > 0) double BuyStopLoss = OpenPrice - (StopLoss * UsePoint);
        if(TakeProfit > 0) double BuyTakeProfit = OpenPrice + (TakeProfit * UsePoint);

        // Open buy order
        BuyTicket = OrderSend(Symbol(),OP_BUY,LotSize,OpenPrice,UseSlippage,
          BuyStopLoss,BuyTakeProfit,"Buy Order",MagicNumber,0,Green);

        SellTicket = 0;
      }


    // Sell Order
    if(FastMA < SlowMA && SellTicket == 0)
      {
        OrderSelect(BuyTicket,SELECT_BY_TICKET);
```

```
            if(OrderCloseTime() == 0 && BuyTicket > 0)
              {
                CloseLots = OrderLots();
                ClosePrice = Bid;

                Closed = OrderClose(BuyTicket,CloseLots,ClosePrice,UseSlippage,Red);
              }

            OpenPrice = Bid;

            if(StopLoss > 0) double SellStopLoss = OpenPrice + (StopLoss * UsePoint);
            if(TakeProfit > 0) double SellTakeProfit = OpenPrice - (TakeProfit * UsePoint);

            SellTicket = OrderSend(Symbol(),OP_SELL,LotSize,OpenPrice,UseSlippage,
              SellStopLoss,SellTakeProfit,"Sell Order",MagicNumber,0,Red);

            BuyTicket = 0;
          }

      return(0);
    }


// Pip Point Function
double PipPoint(string Currency)
  {
    int CalcDigits = MarketInfo(Currency,MODE_DIGITS);
    if(CalcDigits == 2 || CalcDigits == 3) double CalcPoint = 0.01;
    else if(CalcDigits == 4 || CalcDigits == 5) CalcPoint = 0.0001;
    return(CalcPoint);
  }


// Get Slippage Function
int GetSlippage(string Currency, int SlippagePips)
  {
    int CalcDigits = MarketInfo(Currency,MODE_DIGITS);
    if(CalcDigits == 2 || CalcDigits == 4) double CalcSlippage = SlippagePips;
    else if(CalcDigits == 3 || CalcDigits == 5) CalcSlippage = SlippagePips * 10;
    return(CalcSlippage);
  }
```

We start with our **#property copyright** preprocessor directive that identifies the code as belonging to us. The external variables are next, and should be self-explanatory. We declare **BuyTicket** and **SellTicket** as global variables – this way the order ticket is stored between program executions. We could also have declared them as **static** variables within the **start()** function.

We add **UsePoint** and **UseSlippage** as global variables – we'll calculate the value of these next. Our **init()** function is run first. We call the **PipPoint()** and **GetSlippage()** functions (declared at the bottom of the file) and assign the return values to our global variables. We'll use these when referencing point or slippage values in the rest of our expert advisor.

Next is the **start()** function, our main program execution. We've left out **deinit()**, since we have no use for it here. The **iMA()** function calculates the moving average The **FastMA** variable holds our 10 period moving average, which is set using the **FastMAPeriod** variable. The **SlowMA** variable is our 20 period moving average, set using **SlowMAPeriod.** Everything else is set to default (a no shift, simple moving average calculated on the close price).

We use the **if** operator to define our order opening conditions. If the current 10 period moving average (the **FastMA**) is greater than the 20 period moving average (the **SlowMA**), and if **BuyTicket** is equal to 0, we will open a buy order.

Before we open the buy order, we will close the current sell order, if it exists. We use **OrderSelect()** to retrieve the current **SellTicket**. If the order close time is 0 (indicating that the order has not yet been closed), and the **SellTicket** is greater than 0 (indicating that the **SellTicket** is likely valid), we will go ahead and close the sell order. We retrieve the lot size of the sell order and the current **Ask** price, which will be the closing price for the sell order. Then, we close the sell order using **OrderClose()**.

Next, we assign the current **Ask** price to the **OpenPrice** variable – this will be the opening price of our buy order. We calculate our stop loss and take profit relative to the opening price, checking first to make sure that we have specified a **StopLoss** or **TakeProfit** value in the settings. Then, we place the order using the **OrderSend()** function, and store the order ticket in **BuyTicket**. Lastly, we clear the value of **SellTicket**, allowing the placement of another sell order when the order condition becomes valid.

The sell order block follows the same logic as the buy order block. We close the buy order first, and use the **Bid** as the **OpenPrice** and the buy order **ClosePrice**. The stop loss and take profit calculations are reversed.

The **start()** function ends with a **return** operator. Our custom **PipPoint()** and **GetSlippage()** functions are defined at the end after the **start()** function. We will include these functions in every example in this book.

Using Pending Orders

Let's modify our EA to use pending orders. We'll use stop orders in this example. When the fast moving average is greater than the slow moving average, we will place a buy stop order 10 pips above the current high. When the opposite is true, we'll place a sell stop order 10 pips below the current low. Let's declare an external variable to adjust this setting, called **PendingPips**.

```
extern int PendingPips = 10;
```

We're adding the **OrderDelete()** function to our buy and sell order block to close any unfilled pending orders. We need to check the order type of the order indicated by **SellTicket** to ensure that we are using the correct function to close the order.

```
OrderSelect(SellTicket,SELECT_BY_TICKET);

// Close Order
if(OrderCloseTime() == 0 && SellTicket > 0 && OrderType() == OP_SELL)
  {
     double CloseLots = OrderLots();
     double ClosePrice = Ask;

     bool Closed = OrderClose(SellTicket,CloseLots,ClosePrice,UseSlippage,Red);
     if(Closed == true) SellTicket = 0;
  }

// Delete Order
else if(OrderCloseTime() == 0 && SellTicket > 0 && OrderType() == OP_SELLSTOP)
  {
     bool Deleted = OrderDelete(SellTicket,Red);
     if(Deleted == true) SellTicket = 0;
  }
```

We use **OrderType()** to check whether the selected sell order is a market order or a stop order. If it's a market order, we close it using **OrderClose()**. If it's a pending order, we close it using **OrderDelete()**.

Here's our pending order price calculation. We simply convert **PendingPips** to a fractional value with **UsePoint**, and add it to the current **Close** price. We'll store this value in the **PendingPrice** variable. Next, we calculate the stop loss and take profit relative to our pending order price. Finally, we place our pending order using **OrderSend()**, storing the trade result in the variable **BuyTicket**:

```
double PendingPrice = Close[0] + (PendingPips * UsePoint);

if(StopLoss > 0) double BuyStopLoss = PendingPrice - (StopLoss * UsePoint);

if(TakeProfit > 0) double BuyTakeProfit = PendingPrice + (TakeProfit * UsePoint);

BuyTicket = OrderSend(Symbol(),OP_BUYSTOP,LotSize,PendingPrice,UseSlippage,
   BuyStopLoss,BuyTakeProfit,"Buy Stop Order",MagicNumber,0,Green);
```

```
    SellTicket = 0;
```

The code below shows the changes for the sell stop order block:

```
    OrderSelect(BuyTicket,SELECT_BY_TICKET);

    // Close Order
    if(OrderCloseTime() == 0 && BuyTicket > 0 && OrderType() == OP_BUY)
      {
        CloseLots = OrderLots();
        ClosePrice = Bid;

        Closed = OrderClose(BuyTicket,CloseLots,ClosePrice,UseSlippage,Red);
        if(Closed == true) BuyTicket = 0;
      }

    // Delete Order
    else if(OrderCloseTime() == 0 && BuyTicket > 0 && OrderType() == OP_BUYSTOP)
      {
        Closed = OrderDelete(BuyTicket,Red);
        if(Closed == true) BuyTicket = 0;
      }

    PendingPrice = Close[0] - (PendingPips * UsePoint);

    double SellStopLoss = PendingPrice + (StopLoss * UsePoint);
    double SellTakeProfit = PendingPrice - (TakeProfit * UsePoint);

    SellTicket = OrderSend(Symbol(),OP_SELLSTOP,LotSize,PendingPrice,UseSlippage,
      SellStopLoss,SellTakeProfit,"Sell Stop Order",MagicNumber,0,Red);

    BuyTicket = 0;
```

The complete code for both of these expert advisors is in Appendix A.

Chapter 3
Advanced Order Placement

ECN Compatibility

As the order placement examples in the last chapter show, the default method of placing a stop loss and take profit with a market order is to place them using the **OrderSend()** function. While this works well for most brokers, the newer ECN/STP brokers that use MetaTrader don't support this behavior.

In this case, we'll need to place the stop loss and take profit after the order has been placed, using the **OrderModify()** function. This only applies to market orders – for pending orders, you can still place the stop loss and take profit with the **OrderSend()** function.

Order Modification

After placing an order, you can modify the take profit, stop loss, pending order price or expiration time using the **OrderModify()** function. To use **OrderModify()**, we'll need the ticket number of the order that we wish to modify. Here is the syntax for the **OrderModify()** function:

```
bool OrderModify(int Ticket, double Price, double StopLoss, double TakeProfit,
    datetime Expiration, color Arrow = CLR_NONE)
```

- **Ticket** – The ticket number of the order to modify.

- **Price** – The new pending order price.

- **StopLoss** – The new stop loss price.

- **TakeProfit** – The new take profit price.

- **Expiration** – The new expiration time for pending orders.

- **Arrow** – A optional color for the arrow to indicate a modified order. If not indicated, no arrow will be displayed.

If the order modification is successful, **OrderModify()** will return a boolean value of **true**. If the order modification failed, the return value will be **false**.

When modifying orders, we must be sure that the values we are passing to the function are valid. For example, the order must still be open – we cannot modify a closed order. When modifying pending orders with the **Price** parameter, the order must not have already been filled – *i.e.* hit its order price.

The modified order price also must not be too close to the current Bid or Ask price. We should also check to make sure that the stop loss and take profit are valid. We can do this using the price verification routines that we will cover later in this chapter.

If we are not modifying a particular parameter, we must pass the original value to the **OrderModify()** function. For example, if we are modifying only the stop loss for a pending order, then we must retrieve the current order price and take profit using **OrderSelect()** , and pass those values to the **OrderModify()** function.

If you attempt to modify an order without specifying any changed values, you'll get an error 1: "no result". You should verify why your code is passing unchanged values to the function, but otherwise this error is harmless and can be safely ignored.

Adding Stop Loss and Take Profit to an Existing Order

First, we need to verify that the order has been placed correctly. We do this by examining the return value of the **OrderSend()** function, which is the ticket number of the order that was just placed. If the order was not placed due to an error condition, the ticket number will be equal to **-1**.

Next, we use the **OrderSelect()** function to retrieve the information for the order that was just placed. We will use the **OrderOpenPrice(), OrderTakeProfit(), OrderStopLoss()** and optionally the **OrderExpiration()** functions when passing unchanged values to the **OrderModify()** function. Finally, we'll use **OrderModify()** to add the stop loss and take profit to the order.

Here's an example where we set the stop loss and take profit for a buy order using the **OrderModify()** function. We've moved the stop loss and take profit calculation after the **OrderSend()** function, so that it is calculated before we modify the order:

```
int BuyTicket = OrderSend(Symbol(),OP_BUY,LotSize,Ask,UseSlippage,0,0,
  "Buy Order",MagicNumber,0,Green);

if(BuyTicket > 0)
  {
    OrderSelect(BuyTicket,SELECT_BY_TICKET);
    double OpenPrice = OrderOpenPrice();

    if(StopLoss > 0) double BuyStopLoss = OpenPrice - (StopLoss * UsePoint);
    if(TakeProfit > 0) double BuyTakeProfit = OpenPrice + (TakeProfit * UsePoint);
```

```
    if(BuyStopLoss > 0 || BuyTakeProfit > 0)
      {
        bool TicketMod = OrderModify(BuyTicket,OrderOpenPrice(),BuyStopLoss,
          BuyTakeProfit,0);
      }
  }
```

The **OrderSend()** function is identical to our earlier example, except that we use a value of 0 for the stop loss and take profit parameters. A value of zero means that there is no stop loss or take profit being placed with the order. The **BuyTicket** variable stores the ticket number of the order.

We use an **if** statement to check that the **BuyTicket** number is valid – *i.e.* greater than zero. If so, we call the **OrderSelect()** function using our **BuyTicket** number. We retrieve the opening price for the order using **OrderOpenPrice()**, and assign that to the **OpenPrice** variable.

Next, we calculate the stop loss and take profit, relative to the opening price of the order we just placed. We check first to see if the **StopLoss** and **TakeProfit** external variables are greater than zero. If so, we calculate the new stop loss and/or take profit price.

Finally, we call the **OrderModify()** function to add our stop loss and take profit to the order. We check first to make sure that the **BuyStopLoss** or **BuyTakeProfit** variables are something other than zero. If we attempt to modify the order with unchanged values, we'll get an error code 1 from the **OrderModify()** function.

The first parameter for **OrderModify()** is our **BuyTicket** number. We could also use **OrderTicket()** as well. The second parameter is the new order price. Since we are not modifying the order price, we use the **OrderOpenPrice()** function, to indicate that the order price is unchanged.

Remember that we can only modify order prices for pending orders. If we are modifying a market order, we can pass any value for the **Price** parameter, since you cannot change the order price of a market order. But we cannot assume that we will always be modifying market orders, so we will always use **OrderOpenPrice()**.

The **BuyStopLoss** and **BuyTakeProfit** variables pass the changed stop loss and take profit values to the **OrderModify()** function. If you plan on using order expiration times for your pending orders, you can use **OrderExpiration()** as the unchanged Expiration parameter. Otherwise, just use 0.

Although this method adds a few extra steps, we recommended that you use this method of placing stop losses and take profits for market orders in your expert advisors to ensure that they are compatible with all brokers. This method also has the advantage of allowing us to place accurate stop loss and take profit prices without the effects of slippage.

Modifying a Pending Order Price

`OrderModify()` can also be used to modify the order price of a pending order. If the pending order price has already been hit and the order has been filled, it is no longer a pending order, and the price cannot be changed.

We'll use the variable **NewPendingPrice** to represent our changed order price. We'll assume the price has already been calculated and is valid. Here's how we modify a pending order price:

```
OrderSelect(Ticket,SELECT_BY_TICKET);

if(NewPendingPrice != OrderOpenPrice())
   {
     bool TicketMod = OrderModify(Ticket,NewPendingPrice,OrderStopLoss(),
       OrderTakeProfit(),0);
   }
```

As always, we retrieve the order information using `OrderSelect()`. This way we can pass the unchanged stop loss and take profit prices to the `OrderModify()` function. Before modifying the order, we'll check to make sure that our new pending order price is not the same as the current pending order price.

For `OrderModify()`, we specify our order ticket, the new order price stored in **NewPendingPrice**, and the unchanged stop loss and take profit values represented by `OrderStopLoss()` and `OrderTakeProfit()`. We're not using an expiration time for this order, so we use 0 for the expiration parameter.

Verifying Stops and Pending Order Prices

Stop loss, take profit and pending order prices must be a minimum distance away from the Bid and Ask prices. If a stop or pending order price is too close to the current price, an error will result, and the order will not be placed. This is one of the most common trading errors, and it can easily be prevented if the trader is careful to set their stops and pending orders a sufficient distance from the price.

But during periods of rapid price movement, valid stop loss prices can be made invalid by widening spreads. Different brokers have varying stop levels, so a stop loss that is valid on one broker may be too close for another. Some trading systems will set stops and pending order prices based on indicator values, highs or lows, or some other method of calculation where a minimum distance is not guaranteed.

For these reasons, it is always necessary to verify that a stop loss, take profit or pending order price is valid, and not too close to the current market price. We verify this by checking the currency's *stop level.*

Stop Levels

The stop level is the number of pips away from the current Bid or Ask price that all stops and pending orders must be placed. For most brokers, the stop level is approximately 3-4 pips. ECN brokers generally have very tight stop levels, while other brokers such as Alpari have wider stop levels (at least 8 pips).

Figure 3.1 illustrates the stop levels in relation to the prices. Think of the price as not being just a single value (such as the Bid), but rather a thick line the width of the spread.

On either side of that price line are boundaries, indicated by the stop levels. All stop loss, take profit and pending orders must be placed outside of these boundaries.

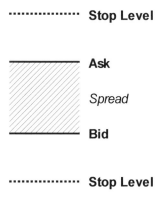

The `MarketInfo()` function with the `MODE_STOPLEVEL` parameter is used to retrieve the stop level for a currency symbol. The stop level is expressed as a whole number, and will need to be converted to a fractional value using `Point`.

Fig. 3.1 – Stop levels

For a 4 digit currency with a stop level of 3 pips, the `MarketInfo()` function with `MODE_STOPLEVEL` will return a 3. For a 5 digit currency with a stop level of 3 pips, `MarketInfo()` will return 30, due to the extra decimal place. Here's the code for retrieving the stop level and converting it to a decimal value:

```
double StopLevel = MarketInfo(Symbol(),MODE_STOPLEVEL) * Point;
```

Note that we use the predefined `Point` variable, instead of the `PipPoint()` function we created earlier. This is because we need to multiply the stop level by the actual point value. For a 4 digit currency, the `Point` will be 0.0001, and for a 5 digit currency, the `Point` will be 0.00001. If the stop level is 3 pips as demonstrated above, then the fractional value will be 0.0003.

Now that we've figured out how to find the stop level, we need to calculate the minimum and maximum values for our stop loss, take profit and pending order prices. We do this by adding or subtracting the stop level from our current Bid and Ask prices.

This code will calculate the minimum allowed price for a buy take profit, sell stop loss, buy stop order, or sell limit order. We'll use the **StopLevel** value we calculated above.

```
double UpperStopLevel = Ask + StopLevel;
```

If our **Ask** price is 1.4650, and the **StopLevel** is 0.0003 pips as calculated above, then the minimum stop level price will be 1.4653. If we are placing a buy take profit with this order, then it must be above this price. We'll call this the **UpperStopLevel**, since it is above the price.

This code will calculate the maximum allowed price for a sell take profit, buy stop loss, sell stop order or sell limit order. Note that we are simply using the **Bid** instead of the **Ask**, and subtracting instead of adding.

```
double LowerStopLevel = Bid - StopLevel;
```

We'll call this the **LowerStopLevel**, since it is below the price. Before placing an order, use the **UpperStopLevel** and **LowerStopLevel** values above to verify your stop loss, take profit and pending order prices. Keep in mind that prices can change rapidly, and you'll want your actual stops, profits and pending orders to be well outside these levels.

Verifying Stop Loss and Take Profit Prices

The minimum take profit in pips will be equal to the order opening price, plus or minus the stop level. If the stop level is 3 pips, and the order opening price is 1.4500, the take profit price for a buy order will need to be above 1.4503.

The minimum stop loss in pips for a market order, however, will include the current spread, so the minimum stop loss will be larger than the minimum take profit. For example, if the stop level is 3 pips, the spread is 2 pips, and the order opening price is 1.4500, the stop loss for a buy market order will need to be below 1.4495.

This doesn't apply for pending orders, so when verifying a stop loss for a pending order, it's not necessary to figure in the spread. So if you're placing a pending order at 1.4500, and the stop level is 3 pips, then the stop loss can be placed anywhere below 1.4497.

Here's an example where we check the stop loss and take profit for a buy order to make sure the prices are valid. If the stop loss or take profit price is not valid, we will automatically adjust it so that it is several pips outside of the stop level.

```
    double MinStop = 5 * UsePoint;

    if(BuyStopLoss > LowerStopLevel) BuyStopLoss = LowerStopLevel - MinStop;
    if(BuyTakeProfit < UpperStopLevel) BuyTakeProfit = UpperStopLevel + MinStop;
```

The variable **MinStop** adds or subtracts 5 pips from the stop level, to ensure that our validated prices do not become invalid due to slippage. You can adjust this value to enforce a sufficient minimum stop/profit level, or even use an external variable to adjust this amount.

The second line compares our stop loss to our **LowerStopLevel**. If the stop loss is greater than our lower stop level, we know that the stop loss is invalid. In that case, we adjust the stop loss to be just a few pips below our stop level. The third line does the same for our take profit.

To check the stop loss and take profit for a sell order, we simply reverse the calculations:

```
    if(SellTakeProfit > LowerStopLevel) SellTakeProfit = LowerStopLevel - MinStop;
    if(SellStopLoss < UpperStopLevel) SellStopLoss = UpperStopLevel + MinStop;
```

Instead of automatically adjusting an invalid price, you could also display an error message and halt program execution. This way the user would be required to readjust their stop loss or take profit setting before continuing. Here's an example of how to do this:

```
    if(BuyStopLoss > LowerStopLevel)
      {
        Alert("The stop loss setting is too small!");
        return(0);
      }
```

If the calculated stop loss is above the stop level, and thus too close to the price, the **Alert()** function will display a pop-up message to the user. The **return** operator exits the current function and assures that the order will not be placed.

In this book, we will be automatically adjusting invalid prices, with the assumption that is is better to place a corrected order than to not place one at all. It may be useful to document when this happens by printing a message to the log:

```
    if(BuyStopLoss > LowerStopLevel)
      {
        BuyStopLoss = LowerStopLevel - MinStop;
        Print("Stop loss is invalid and has been automatically adjusted");
      }
```

Verifying Pending Order Prices

Here's how we verify the pending order price for a buy stop or sell limit order. The **PendingPrice** variable stores our pending order price:

```
if(PendingPrice < UpperStopLevel) PendingPrice = UpperStopLevel + MinStop;
```

Notice that the logic here is identical to the code above that checks our buy take profit and sell stop loss prices. And here's the code to check the pending order price for a sell stop or buy limit order:

```
if(PendingPrice > UpperStopLevel) PendingPrice = UpperStopLevel — MinStop;
```

Calculating Lot Size

Aside from choosing suitable stop loss and take profit levels, using an appropriate lot size is one of the best risk management tools you have. Specifying a lot size can be as simple as declaring an external variable and using a fixed lot size for every order. In this section, we'll explore a more sophisticated method that calculates the lot size based on the maximum amount you're willing to lose per trade.

Over-leveraging is one of the big killers of forex traders. Using lot sizes that are too large in relation to your equity can wipe out your account just as easily as it can produce big gains. It is recommended that you use no more than 2-3% of your equity per trade. By this, we mean that the maximum amount you can lose per trade will be no more that 2-3% of your account.

Money Management

To calculate the lot size using this method, we need to specify a percentage of equity to use and the stop loss in pips. We'll use the external variable **EquityPercent** to set the percentage of equity to use. We'll assume a stop loss of 50 pips is used.

```
extern double EquityPercent = 2;
extern double StopLoss = 50;
```

First, we need to calculate the amount of equity specified by **EquityPercent**. If we have a balance of $10,000, and we are using 2% of our equity, then the calculation is as follows:

```
double RiskAmount = AccountEquity() * (EquityPercent / 100);
```

`AccountEquity()` is an MQL function that returns the current account equity. We divide `EquityPercent` by 100 to give us a fractional value (0.02). Then, we multiply that by `AccountEquity()` to calculate the amount of equity to use. 2% of $10,000 is $200, and this will be stored in the variable `RiskAmount`.

Next, we have to find the *tick value*. This is the profit per pip if we were trading one lot of the desired currency. For example, if we are trading 1 lot of EURUSD on a standard account (100k lots), the profit per pip would be $10. On a mini account (10k lots), the profit per pip would be $1.

We can use the `MarketInfo()` function with the `MODE_TICKVALUE` parameter to return the profit per pip for the specified currency. The tick value must be in pips, so if we are trading on a fractional pip broker (3 or 5 decimal places), we must multiply the tick value by 10.

```
double TickValue = MarketInfo(Symbol(),MODE_TICKVALUE);
if(Point == 0.001 || Point == 0.00001) TickValue *= 10;
```

Assuming we are trading a standard account, the tick value for EURUSD will be 10. This will be stored in the `TickValue` variable. If this is a fractional pip broker, then `TickValue` will be 1. We will need to multiply this by 10 to make it equivalent to one pip. If the `Point` variable indicates that the currency is 3 or 5 decimal places, then `TickValue` will be multiplied by 10 to make it equal to a 2 or 4 decimal place value.

The next step is to calculate our lot size. First, we divide the `RiskAmount` by the `StopLoss` setting. This will give us our profit per tick for this order. $200 divided by our stop loss of 50 will give us $4. Now all we have to do is divide that by `TickValue` to get the lot size:

```
double CalcLots = (RiskAmount / StopLoss) / TickValue;
```

Our calculated lot size on a standard account will be 0.4 lots. On a mini account, the calculated lot size will be 4 lots. This value is stored in the `CalcLots` variable.

If you are using proper money management, the percentage of equity you are using will be fairly consistent. (1-2% for conservative risk, up to 5% for higher risk). Your stop loss, on the other hand, will vary based on your time frame and your trading system. The lot size will vary widely depending on your stop loss.

A tight stop loss will generate a larger lot size, which provides a lot of upside benefit if your order hits its take profit. On the other hand, if you're using a large stop loss, your lot size will be fairly small. This method will benefit best from using fairly tight stops and/or large take profit values.

If you must use a large stop loss, or none at all, a fixed lot size would probably be more beneficial. We need to be able to choose between calculating the lot size or using a fixed lot size. Let's use an external boolean variable called **DynamicLotSize** to turn our lot size calculation on and off:

```
// External variables
extern bool DynamicLotSize = true;
extern double EquityPercent = 2;
extern double FixedLotSize = 0.1;


// Start function
if(DynamicLotSize == true)
  {
    double RiskAmount = AccountEquity() * (EquityPercent / 100);
    double TickValue = MarketInfo(Symbol(),MODE_TICKVALUE);
    if(Digits == 3 || Digits == 5) TickValue *= 10;
    double CalcLots = (RiskAmount / StopLoss) / TickValue;
    double LotSize = CalcLots;
  }
else LotSize = FixedLotSize;
```

If **DynamicLotSize** is set to true, we will calculate the lot size based on the stop loss, and assign that value to the **LotSize** variable. If **DynamicLotSize** is false, we simply assign the value of **FixedLotSize** to **LotSize**. The **LotSize** variable will be passed to the **OrderSend()** function as the lot size for the order.

Verifying Lot Size

Just like the stop loss, take profit and pending order prices, the lot size should also be verified to make sure it is acceptable to your broker. This means that your lot size should not be too large or too small, and it should not be specified in micro lots (0.01) if your broker doesn't support those. You should also normalize your lot size to the appropriate decimal place.

Let's check the minimum and maximum lot size first. The **MarketInfo()** function, using the **MODE_MINLOT** and **MODE_MAXLOT** parameters, will be used to compare the current lot size to the minimum and maximum lot size. If the lot size is not valid, it will automatically be resized to the minimum or maximum.

```
if(LotSize < MarketInfo(Symbol(),MODE_MINLOT))
  {
    LotSize = MarketInfo(Symbol(),MODE_MINLOT);
  }
```

```
    else if(LotSize > MarketInfo(Symbol(),MODE_MAXLOT))
      {
        LotSize = MarketInfo(Symbol(),MODE_MAXLOT);
      }
```

We simply compare the value of **LotSize**, our calculated or fixed lot size from above, to the minimum and maximum lot size. If **LotSize** is less than the minimum lot size, or greater than the maximum lot size, it will be assigned the appropriate minimum or maximum value.

Next, we need to compare our lot size to the *step value*. The step value indicates whether the broker allows micro lots (0.01) or mini lots (0.1). If you attempt to use a micro lot size on a broker that only allows mini lots, you will get an error and the trade will not be placed. Here's the code to check the step value:

```
    if(MarketInfo(Symbol(),MODE_LOTSTEP) == 0.1)
      {
        LotSize = NormalizeDouble(LotSize,1);
      }
    else LotSize = NormalizeDouble(LotSize,2);
```

The **NormalizeDouble()** function rounds the value of **LotSize** to the number of digits specified in the second argument. In the first line, if the step size is 0.1, indicating the the broker only uses mini lots, **LotSize** will be rounded to one decimal place. Otherwise, **LotSize** will be rounded to 2 decimal places.

If in the future you happen to come across a broker that allows lot sizes up to three decimal places, then you could easily modify the above code to check that as well. But at moment, virtually every MetaTrader broker uses either one or two decimal places for lot sizing.

Other Considerations

Trade Context

MetaTrader has a single trade execution thread for expert advisors. This means that only one expert advisor can trade at any one time, regardless of how many expert advisors are running in the terminal. Before commencing with any trade operations, we must check to see whether the trade execution thread is currently being used.

The function **IsTradeContextBusy()** will return true if the trade execution thread is occupied, otherwise false. We will call this function just before calling any trading functions, including **OrderSend()**, **OrderClose()**, **OrderDelete()** or **OrderModify()**.

Here's how we check the trading execution thread using **IsTradeContextBusy()**:

```
while(IsTradeContextBusy()) Sleep(10);

int Ticket = OrderSend(Symbol(),OP_BUY,LotSize,Ask,UseSlippage,0,0,
   "Buy Order",MagicNumber,0,Green);
```

We use a **while** loop to evaluate **IsTradeContextBusy()**. If the function returns true, indicating that the trade execution thread is occupied, the expert advisor will **Sleep** for 10 milliseconds. The **while** loop will continue to execute as long as **IsTradeContextBusy()** returns true. Once the trade thread is freed up, trading will commence.

If the expert advisor attempts to trade while the trade execution thread is occupied, an error 147 : "trade context busy" will result. Although this method is fairly reliable at avoiding the "trade context busy" error, it is not foolproof, especially when multiple expert advisors are attempting to trade at the same time. Later in the book, we will explore ways to retry trade operations after certain error conditions.

Refreshing Predefined Variables

The values of predefined variables such as **Bid** and **Ask** are set when the expert advisor begins its execution. The amount of time required to execute our expert advisor code is very short, and can be measured in milliseconds. But when you figure in delays for trade server response, and the fact that prices can change very rapidly, it's very important that you always use the most current prices.

The **RefreshRates()** function updates the contents of predefined variables with the latest prices from the server. It is recommended that you call this function every time you use the **Bid** or **Ask** variables, especially after a prior trade execution.

Note that if you retrieve the price using the **MarketInfo()** function, it is not necessary to use **RefreshRates()**. We covered **MarketInfo()** on page 29. When we get to the chapter on creating functions, we will use **MarketInfo()** to retrieve prices instead of using predefined variables. However, you may still want to use **Bid** and **Ask** in your **start()** function to reference the current chart prices.

Error Handling

When placing, modifying or closing orders, errors can occur due to invalid trade parameters, requotes, or server issues. We've done our best to make sure that the trade parameters we use are valid and have been checked to prevent common, preventable errors. But when errors do occur, we need to alert the user of the error and log any relevant information for troubleshooting.

We check for possible errors by examining the output of functions such as **OrderSend()**, **OrderModify()** and **OrderClose()**. If the function did not complete successfully, the function will return **-1** for **OrderSend()**, or **false** for **OrderModify()** and **OrderClose()**.

In this section, we will create an error handling routine for the **OrderSend()** function. If the return value of **OrderSend()** is -1, we will run an error handling routine to display an alert to the user, and print relevant trade parameter and price information to the log.

First, we must first retrieve the error code. This is done using the **GetLastError()** function. We need to store the return value of **GetLastError()** in a variable, because once **GetLastError()** has been called, the error code will be cleared and the next call of **GetLastError()** will return 0. We'll declare a global variable called **ErrorCode** and use it to store the value of **GetLastError()**.

Next, we'll need to get some descriptive information on the error. The include file **stdlib.mqh** contains a function called **ErrorDescription()**. This function returns a string with a description of the error. It's actually not very descriptive, but it's better than nothing. We'll need to add an **#include** statement for **stdlib.mqh** at the top of our file.

Then we'll print an alert to the user's screen using the built-in **Alert()** function. This information will also be printed to the log. The alert will include the error code, the error description, and a short description of the operation we just attempted to carry out. This way you'll know exactly which section in your program generated the error.

Finally, we will print relevant price information to the log using the **Print()** function. Along with the current Bid & Ask prices, we will include trade parameters such as the lot size and the order price.

```
// Preprocessor section
#include <stdlib.mqh>

// Global variable
int ErrorCode;

// Order placement
int Ticket = OrderSend(Symbol(),OP_BUYSTOP,LotSize,PendingPrice,UseSlippage,0,0,
  "Buy Stop Order",MagicNumber,0,Green);

if(Ticket == -1)
  {
    ErrorCode = GetLastError();
    string ErrDesc = ErrorDescription(ErrorCode);

    string ErrAlert = StringConcatenate("Open Buy Stop Order - Error ",
      ErrorCode,": ",ErrDesc);
    Alert(ErrAlert);
```

```
    string ErrLog = StringConcatenate("Bid: ",Bid," Ask: ",Ask," Price: ",
        PendingPrice," Lots: ",LotSize);
    Print(ErrLog);
}
```

At the top, we include the **stdlib.mqh** file. We add the **ErrorCode** global variable to store our error code. The **OrderSend()** places a buy stop order. If the function is not successful, our error handling code is run.

First, we store the value of **GetLastError()** in **ErrorCode**. Then we call the **ErrorDescription()** function, using **ErrorCode** as the argument. Next, we use the **StringConcatenate()** function to create our alert message, which is stored in the string variable **ErrAlert**.

StringConcatenate() is an MQL function that allows you to create complex strings using variables and constants. Each string element to be joined (or "concatenated") together is separated by a comma. Try typing the examples above into MetaEditor to view it with syntax highlighting.

You can also concatenate strings by combining them with a plus sign (+). Using **StringConcatenate()** is clearer and more efficient, but if you want to simply concatenate a short string, use the plus sign to combine string constants and variables:

```
    string PlusCat = "The current Ask price is "+Ask;
    // Sample output: The current Ask price is 1.4320
```

The **Alert()** function displays a pop-up on the user's desktop, containing the contents of the **ErrAlert** variable. Figure 3.2 displays the output of the **Alert()** function.

We construct another string with our price and trade parameters, and store it in the **ErrLog** variable, which we pass to the **Print()** function. **Print()** prints the contents of the function argument to the experts log. The experts log can be viewed from the *Experts* tab inside the *Terminal* window, or from the *Journal* tab in the *Tester* window if you're using the Strategy Tester.

Fig. 3.2 – Alert message

Here are the log contents. The first line is the output from the **Alert()** function. The second line is the output of the **Print()** function. Notice the error, "invalid trade volume", and the fact that the lot size reported in the log is 0. In this case, the problem is that the lot size is invalid.

```
16:47:54 Profit Buster EURUSD,H1: Alert: Open Buy Stop Order - Error 131:
    invalid trade volume

16:47:54 Profit Buster EURUSD,H1: Bid: 1.5046, Ask: 1.5048, Lots: 0
```

You can create similar error handling routines for other functions as well, especially for the **OrderModify()** and **OrderClose()** functions. You can also create more sophisticated error handling routines that provide custom error messages based on the error code, or perform other actions.

For example, if you receive error 130: "invalid stops", you could display a message such as "The stop loss or take profit price is invalid." Here's an example of how you can do this:

```
ErrorCode = GetLastError();

string ErrDesc;
if(ErrorCode == 129) ErrDesc = "Order opening price is invalid!";
if(ErrorCode == 130) ErrDesc = "Stop loss or take profit is invalid!";
if(ErrorCode == 131) ErrDesc = "Lot size is invalid!";

string ErrAlert = StringConcatenate("Open Buy Order - Error ",ErrorCode,": ",ErrDesc);
Alert(ErrAlert);
```

Putting It All Together

We're going to add all of the features we've covered in this section to the simple expert advisor we created on page 36. We'll be adding order modification, stop level verification, trade context checking, predefined variable refreshing and lot size verification to our EA. Here is our file, starting at the beginning:

```
#property copyright "Andrew Young"
#include <stdlib.mqh>


// External variables
extern bool DynamicLotSize = true;
extern double EquityPercent = 2;
extern double FixedLotSize = 0.1;

extern double StopLoss = 50;
extern double TakeProfit = 100;

extern int Slippage = 5;
extern int MagicNumber = 123;

extern int FastMAPeriod = 10;
extern int SlowMAPeriod = 20;


// Global variables
int BuyTicket;
int SellTicket;

double UsePoint;
int UseSlippage;

int ErrorCode;
```

We've added the **#include** statement for the **stdlib.mqh** file that contains the **ErrorDescription()** function for our error handling routines. We've added three external variables for the lot sizing, and a global variable for the error code.

The following code goes at the beginning of the **start()** function:

```
// Moving averages
double FastMA = iMA(NULL,0,FastMAPeriod,0,0,0,0);
double SlowMA = iMA(NULL,0,SlowMAPeriod,0,0,0,0);
```

```
// Lot size calculation
if(DynamicLotSize == true)
  {
     double RiskAmount = AccountEquity() * (EquityPercent / 100);
     double TickValue = MarketInfo(Symbol(),MODE_TICKVALUE);
     if(Point == 0.001 || Point == 0.00001) TickValue *= 10;
     double CalcLots = (RiskAmount / StopLoss) / TickValue;
     double LotSize = CalcLots;
  }
else LotSize = FixedLotSize;


// Lot size verification
if(LotSize < MarketInfo(Symbol(),MODE_MINLOT))
  {
     LotSize = MarketInfo(Symbol(),MODE_MINLOT);
  }

else if(LotSize > MarketInfo(Symbol(),MODE_MAXLOT))
  {
     LotSize = MarketInfo(Symbol(),MODE_MAXLOT);
  }

if(MarketInfo(Symbol(),MODE_LOTSTEP) == 0.1)
  {
     LotSize = NormalizeDouble(LotSize,1);
  }
else LotSize = NormalizeDouble(LotSize,2);
```

The lot size calculation and verification code from page 51 is added to the beginning of our start function. Since our stop loss level is known beforehand, this is a good a place as any to put it. The remaining code is our modified buy market order routine:

```
// Buy Order
if(FastMA > SlowMA && BuyTicket == 0)
  {
     // Close Order
     OrderSelect(SellTicket,SELECT_BY_TICKET);

     if(OrderCloseTime() == 0 && SellTicket > 0)
       {
          double CloseLots = OrderLots();

          while(IsTradeContextBusy()) Sleep(10);

          RefreshRates();
          double ClosePrice = Ask;

          bool Closed = OrderClose(SellTicket,CloseLots,ClosePrice,UseSlippage,Red);
```

```
     // Error handling
     if(Closed == false)
       {
          ErrorCode = GetLastError();
          string ErrDesc = ErrorDescription(ErrorCode);

          string ErrAlert = StringConcatenate("Close Sell Order - Error ",
            ErrorCode,": ",ErrDesc);
          Alert(ErrAlert);

          string ErrLog = StringConcatenate("Ask: ",Ask," Lots: ",LotSize,
            " Ticket: ",SellTicket);
          Print(ErrLog);
       }
  }


// Open buy order
while(IsTradeContextBusy()) Sleep(10);
RefreshRates();

BuyTicket = OrderSend(Symbol(),OP_BUY,LotSize,Ask,UseSlippage,0,0,
  "Buy Order",MagicNumber,0,Green);

// Error handling
if(BuyTicket == -1)
  {
     ErrorCode = GetLastError();
     ErrDesc = ErrorDescription(ErrorCode);
     ErrAlert = StringConcatenate("Open Buy Order - Error ",
       ErrorCode,": ",ErrDesc);
     Alert(ErrAlert);

     ErrLog = StringConcatenate("Ask: ",Ask," Lots: ",LotSize);
     Print(ErrLog);
  }

// Order modification
else
  {
     OrderSelect(BuyTicket,SELECT_BY_TICKET);
     double OpenPrice = OrderOpenPrice();

     // Calculate stop level
     double StopLevel = MarketInfo(Symbol(),MODE_STOPLEVEL) * Point;

     RefreshRates();
     double UpperStopLevel = Ask + StopLevel;
     double LowerStopLevel = Bid - StopLevel;

     double MinStop = 5 * UsePoint;
```

```
    // Calculate stop loss and take profit
    if(StopLoss > 0) double BuyStopLoss = OpenPrice - (StopLoss * UsePoint);
    if(TakeProfit > 0) double BuyTakeProfit = OpenPrice + (TakeProfit * UsePoint);

    // Verify stop loss and take profit
    if(BuyStopLoss > 0 && BuyStopLoss > LowerStopLevel)
      {
        BuyStopLoss = LowerStopLevel - MinStop;
      }

    if(BuyTakeProfit > 0 && BuyTakeProfit < UpperStopLevel)
      {
        BuyTakeProfit = UpperStopLevel + MinStop;
      }

    // Modify order
    if(IsTradeContextBusy()) Sleep(10);

    if(BuyStopLoss > 0 || BuyTakeProfit > 0)
      {
        bool TicketMod = OrderModify(BuyTicket,OpenPrice,BuyStopLoss,
          BuyTakeProfit,0);

        // Error handling
        if(TicketMod == false)
          {
            ErrorCode = GetLastError();
            ErrDesc = ErrorDescription(ErrorCode);
            ErrAlert = StringConcatenate("Modify Buy Order - Error ",
              ErrorCode,": ",ErrDesc);
            Alert(ErrAlert);

            ErrLog = StringConcatenate("Ask: ",Ask," Bid: ",Bid," Ticket: ",
              BuyTicket," Stop: ",BuyStopLoss," Profit: ",BuyTakeProfit);
            Print(ErrLog);
          }
      }
  }

SellTicket = 0;
}
```

The remainder of our code contains the sell market order placement block, as well as the **PipPoint()** and **GetSlippage()** functions. You can view the full code for this expert advisor in Appendix B.

Note that we've added the **IsTradeContextBusy()** function prior to every trade operation. We want to make sure that the trade thread is free before attempting to trade. We use the **RefreshRates()**

function before each reference of the **Bid** or **Ask** variables, to ensure that we are always using the latest prices.

We begin by selecting the previous sell order ticket and closing it using **OrderClose()**. If the function fails, the error handling block is run. Next, we open the buy market order using **OrderSend()**. If the function fails, it's error handling block is run. Otherwise, we continue to the order modification block.

We select the order that was just placed using **OrderSelect()**, and assign the order's opening price to the **OpenPrice** variable. We then calculate the stop level and the upper and lower stop level prices. Next, we calculate our stop loss and take profit prices, verify those, and finally we modify the order using **OrderModify()**. A final error handling block deals with errors from the order modification.

Here's how we modify the code for a pending buy stop order:

```
// Close order
OrderSelect(SellTicket,SELECT_BY_TICKET);

if(OrderCloseTime() == 0 && SellTicket > 0 && OrderType() == OP_SELL)
   {
      double CloseLots = OrderLots();

      while(IsTradeContextBusy()) Sleep(10);

      RefreshRates();
      double ClosePrice = Ask;

      bool Closed = OrderClose(SellTicket,CloseLots,ClosePrice,UseSlippage,Red);

      // Error handling
      if(Closed == false)
        {
          ErrorCode = GetLastError();
          string ErrDesc = ErrorDescription(ErrorCode);

          string ErrAlert = StringConcatenate("Close Sell Order - Error ",ErrorCode,
            ": ",ErrDesc);
          Alert(ErrAlert);

          string ErrLog = StringConcatenate("Ask: ",Ask," Lots: ",LotSize,
            " Ticket: ",SellTicket);
          Print(ErrLog);
       }
   }
```

```
    // Delete order
    else if(OrderCloseTime() == 0 && SellTicket > 0 && OrderType() == OP_SELLSTOP)
      {
        bool Deleted = OrderDelete(SellTicket,Red);
        if(Deleted == true) SellTicket = 0;

        // Error handling
        if(Deleted == false)
          {
            ErrorCode = GetLastError();
            ErrDesc = ErrorDescription(ErrorCode);

            ErrAlert = StringConcatenate("Delete Sell Stop Order - Error ",ErrorCode,
              ": ",ErrDesc);
            Alert(ErrAlert);

            ErrLog = StringConcatenate("Ask: ",Ask," Ticket: ",SellTicket);
            Print(ErrLog);
          }
      }
```

We've added the code to delete pending orders using **OrderDelete()** after the **OrderClose()** function. The order type of the previous sell order determines which function is used to close the order.

The main difference between the following code and the market order code is that we do not have an order modification block. It is not necessary to place the stop loss and take profit separately for pending orders. Therefore we will calculate the stop loss and take profit before placing the order with **OrderSend()**.

```
    // Calculate stop level
    double StopLevel = MarketInfo(Symbol(),MODE_STOPLEVEL) * Point;
    RefreshRates();
    double UpperStopLevel = Ask + StopLevel;
    double MinStop = 5 * UsePoint;

    // Calculate pending price
    double PendingPrice = High[0] + (PendingPips * UsePoint);
    if(PendingPrice < UpperStopLevel) PendingPrice = UpperStopLevel + MinStop;

    // Calculate stop loss and take profit
    if(StopLoss > 0) double BuyStopLoss = PendingPrice - (StopLoss * UsePoint);
    if(TakeProfit > 0) double BuyTakeProfit = PendingPrice + (TakeProfit * UsePoint);

    // Verify stop loss and take profit
    UpperStopLevel = PendingPrice + StopLevel;
    double LowerStopLevel = PendingPrice - StopLevel;
```

```
   if(BuyStopLoss > 0 && BuyStopLoss > LowerStopLevel)
     {
        BuyStopLoss = LowerStopLevel - MinStop;
     }

   if(BuyTakeProfit  > 0 && BuyTakeProfit < UpperStopLevel)
     {
        BuyTakeProfit = UpperStopLevel + MinStop;
     }

   // Place pending order
   if(IsTradeContextBusy()) Sleep(10);

   BuyTicket = OrderSend(Symbol(),OP_BUYSTOP,LotSize,PendingPrice,UseSlippage,
     BuyStopLoss,BuyTakeProfit,"Buy Stop Order",MagicNumber,0,Green);

   // Error handling
   if(BuyTicket == -1)
     {
       ErrorCode = GetLastError();
       ErrDesc = ErrorDescription(ErrorCode);

       ErrAlert = StringConcatenate("Open Buy Stop Order - Error ",ErrorCode,
         ": ",ErrDesc);
       Alert(ErrAlert);

       ErrLog = StringConcatenate("Ask: ",Ask," Lots: ",LotSize," Price: ",PendingPrice,
         " Stop: ",BuyStopLoss," Profit: ",BuyTakeProfit);
       Print(ErrLog);
     }

   SellTicket = 0;
```

First, we calculate the upper stop level. We then calculate and verify our pending order price, which is stored in **PendingPrice**. We then recalculate **UpperStopLevel** and calculate the **LowerStopLevel** so that they are relative to the pending order price. Note that we do not need to use the Ask or Bid prices, or figure in the spread when verifying the stop loss and take profit prices.

Finally, we place our pending order using **OrderSend()**, placing the stop loss and take profit along with it. We have the standard error handling function to deal with order placement errors.

Despite all the extra code, these expert advisors are using the same strategy as the one at the end of chapter 2. This code simply has extra features for calculating and verifying lot size, stop levels, stop loss, take profit and pending order prices. We've also added trade context checks and error handling code. In the next chapter, we'll learn how to create functions so we can reuse and simplify this code.

Chapter 4
Working with Functions

We're going to convert the code that we've discussed in the previous chapters into reusable functions. This will save us a lot of work, as we can focus on the details of our trading system instead of the mechanics of trading.

The idea behind creating functions is to create a block of code that carries out a very specific task. The code should be flexible enough to be reused in a variety of trading situations. Any external variables or calculations will need to be passed to the function. We can't assume that any necessary values will be available to our function otherwise, since the function may reside in an external include file or library.

For consistency, we will keep the same names for any external variables that we have used so far. We'll preface these variables with "**arg**", to indicate that they are function arguments.

Lot Sizing Function

Let's start with our lot size calculation, as defined on page 51:

```
double CalcLotSize(bool argDynamicLotSize, double argEquityPercent, double argStopLoss,
  double argFixedLotSize)
  {
    if(argDynamicLotSize == true)
      {
        double RiskAmount = AccountEquity() * (argEquityPercent / 100);
        double TickValue = MarketInfo(Symbol(),MODE_TICKVALUE);
        if(Point == 0.001 || Point == 0.00001) TickValue *= 10;
        double LotSize = (RiskAmount / argStopLoss) / TickValue;
      }
    else LotSize = argFixedLotSize;

    return(LotSize);
  }
```

The first line is our function declaration. We call this function **CalcLotSize()**. Compare this to the code on page 51. Notice that **DynamicLotSize**, **EquityPercent**, **StopLoss** and **FixedLotSize** are all function arguments now. The external variables with these names still exist in our program, we will just pass them to the function as arguments now.

The arguments to our function are highlighted in bold. Other than the fact that we're using arguments now, the code is identical to the lot size calculation code from earlier. We've added a **return** statement at the end of the function – this will return the value of **LotSize** to our calling function.

The function itself will be placed somewhere in our program file, outside of the **start()** and **init()** functions, or it will be located in an external include file. In the latter case, an **#include** statement at the top of the program would include the file for use in our program.

Here's how we would use this function in code. First, let's list the external variables we'll use for our lot size settings:

```
extern bool DynamicLotSize = true;
extern double EquityPercent = 2;
extern double FixedLotSize = 0.1;
extern double StopLoss = 50;
```

And here's how we call the function. This line of code would be located inside the **start()** function:

```
double LotSize = CalcLotSize(DynamicStopLoss,EquityPercent,StopLoss,FixedLotSize);
```

Our external variables are passed to the function as arguments. The function will calculate our lot size, and the value will be saved in the variable **LotSize**. Note that this variable is different from the **LotSize** variable that is inside the **CalcLotSize()** function. Both variables are local to their functions, so even though they have the same name, they are not the same variable.

Lot Verification Function

Let's continue with the lot verification code from page 51. This will be a separate function, in case you decide to use an alternate method of calculating lot size. Regardless of the method of determining lot size, you'll want to verify it before using passing it to an order placement function:

```
double VerifyLotSize(double argLotSize)
  {
    if(argLotSize < MarketInfo(Symbol(),MODE_MINLOT))
      {
        argLotSize = MarketInfo(Symbol(),MODE_MINLOT);
      }
    else if(argLotSize > MarketInfo(Symbol(),MODE_MAXLOT))
      {
        argLotSize = MarketInfo(Symbol(),MODE_MAXLOT);
      }
```

```
      if(MarketInfo(Symbol(),MODE_LOTSTEP) == 0.1)
        {
          argLotSize = NormalizeDouble(argLotSize,1);
        }
      else argLotSize = NormalizeDouble(argLotSize,2);

      return(argLotSize);
    }
```

For this function, we'll pass the variable with the lot size we calculated using **CalcLotSize()** as the argument. The argument variable **argLotSize** is then processed and returned back to the calling function.

Order Placement Function

Now it's time to assemble our buy market order placement function. There will be a few differences between our order placement function and the code we reviewed earlier. For one, we will not be closing orders in our order placement functions. We will handle the closing of orders separately. We'll create a function to close orders in the next chapter.

We will also be calculating and modifying our stop loss and take profit prices outside of the order placement function. Because there are multiple ways of calculating stops, we need to keep our order placement function as flexible as possible, and not tie it to a predetermined method of calculating stops. The order modification code has been moved to a separate function.

We'll place our buy order at the current market price using **OrderSend()**, and if the order was not placed, we'll run the error handling code from page 54. In any case, we'll return the ticket number to the calling function, or **-1** if the order was not placed.

We are specifying the order symbol using the **argSymbol** argument, instead of simply using the current chart symbol. This way, if you decide to place an order on another symbol, you can do so easily. Instead of using the predefined **Bid** and **Ask** variables, we'll need to use the **MarketInfo()** function with the **MODE_ASK** and **MODE_BID** parameters to retrieve the Bid and Ask price for that particular symbol.

We have also specified a default value for the order comment. The argument **argComment** has a default value, **"Buy Order"**. If no value is specified for this argument, then the default is used. We'll assume that the lot size and slippage have been calculated and verified prior to calling this function:

```
int OpenBuyOrder(string argSymbol, double argLotSize, double argSlippage,
   double argMagicNumber, string argComment = "Buy Order")
  {
    while(IsTradeContextBusy()) Sleep(10);

    // Place Buy Order
    int Ticket = OrderSend(argSymbol,OP_BUY,argLotSize,MarketInfo(argSymbol,MODE_ASK),
      argSlippage,0,0,argComment,argMagicNumber,0,Green);

    // Error Handling
    if(Ticket == -1)
      {
        int ErrorCode = GetLastError();
        string ErrDesc = ErrorDescription(ErrorCode);

        string ErrAlert = StringConcatenate("Open Buy Order - Error ",
          ErrorCode,": ",ErrDesc);
        Alert(ErrAlert);

        string ErrLog = StringConcatenate("Bid: ",MarketInfo(argSymbol,MODE_BID),
          " Ask: ",MarketInfo(argSymbol,MODE_ASK)," Lots: ",argLotSize);
        Print(ErrLog);
      }

    return(Ticket);
  }
```

In the **OrderSend()** function, note that we've used the **MarketInfo()** function with the **MODE_ASK** parameter, in place of the predefined **Ask** variable. This will retrieve the current Ask price for the currency symbol indicated by **argSymbol**.

If the trade was not placed successfully, the error handling routine will be run. Otherwise the order ticket will be returned to the calling function, or **-1** if the order was not placed. The complete order placement function for sell market orders is in Appendix D.

Pending Order Placement

To place pending orders, we'll need to pass parameters for the pending order price as well as the order expiration time. The **argPendingPrice** and **argExpiration** arguments will be added to the function.

We'll assume that the pending order price, as well as the stop loss and take profit, have been calculated and verified prior to calling this function. The pending order placement functions will place the stop loss and take profit with the pending order, so no separate order modification function is required.

Here's the code to place a pending buy stop order:

```
int OpenBuyStopOrder(string argSymbol, double argLotSize, double argPendingPrice,
  double argStopLoss, double argTakeProfit, double argSlippage, double argMagicNumber,
  datetime argExpiration = 0, string argComment = "Buy Stop Order")
  {
    while(IsTradeContextBusy()) Sleep(10);

    // Place Buy Stop Order
    int Ticket = OrderSend(argSymbol,OP_BUYSTOP,argLotSize,argPendingPrice,
      argSlippage,argStopLoss,argTakeProfit,argComment,argMagicNumber,
      argExpiration,Green);

    // Error Handling
    if(Ticket == -1)
      {
        int ErrorCode = GetLastError();
        string ErrDesc = ErrorDescription(ErrorCode);

        string ErrAlert = StringConcatenate("Open Buy Stop Order - Error ",ErrorCode,
          ": ",ErrDesc);
        Alert(ErrAlert);

        string ErrLog = StringConcatenate("Ask: ",MarketInfo(argSymbol,MODE_ASK),
          " Lots: ",argLotSize," Price: ",argPendingPrice," Stop: ",argStopLoss,
          " Profit: ",argTakeProfit," Expiration: ",TimeToStr(argExpiration));
        Print(ErrLog);
      }

    return(Ticket);
  }
```

Note that we've specified a default value of 0 for **argExpiration**. If you are not using a pending order expiration time, and you wish to use the default order comment, you can simply omit the arguments for **argExpiration** and **argComment** when calling the function. The following example will place a buy stop order with no expiration time and the default order comment, "Buy Stop Order":

```
int Ticket = OpenBuyStopOrder(Symbol(),LotSize,PendingPrice,StopLoss,TakeProfit,
  UseSlippage,MagicNumber);
```

We've added the pending price to the log in our error handling function, as well as the expiration time, if one is specified. The **TimeToStr()** function converts a datetime variable to a readable string format.

The functions to open sell stop, buy limit and sell limit orders are identical to this one. The only difference is that the order type parameter for the **OrderSend()** function is changed accordingly. You can view all of the pending order placement functions in Appendix D.

Order Closing Function

Lastly, let's create a function for closing a single order. We'll use the order closing block from the code on page 58. In the next chapter, we'll examine ways of closing multiple orders of the same type, which is a simpler method of closing orders. But in case you need to close just one order, this function will do the trick:

```
bool CloseBuyOrder(string argSymbol, int argCloseTicket, double argSlippage)
   {
      OrderSelect(argCloseTicket,SELECT_BY_TICKET);

    if(OrderCloseTime() == 0)
       {
          double CloseLots = OrderLots();

          while(IsTradeContextBusy()) Sleep(10);

          double ClosePrice = MarketInfo(argSymbol,MODE_ASK);

          bool Closed = OrderClose(argCloseTicket,CloseLots,ClosePrice,argSlippage,Red);

          if(Closed == false)
            {
               int ErrorCode = GetLastError();
               string ErrDesc = ErrorDescription(ErrorCode);

               string ErrAlert = StringConcatenate("Close Buy Order -  Error: ",ErrorCode,
                  ": ",ErrDesc);
               Alert(ErrAlert);

               string ErrLog = StringConcatenate("Ticket: ",argCloseTicket," Ask: ",
                  MarketInfo(argSymbol,MODE_ASK));
               Print(ErrLog);
            }
       }

    return(Closed);
   }
```

For the **ClosePrice** variable, we use **MarketInfo()** to retrieve the current Ask price for the currency indicated by **argSymbol**. We use the function arguments **argCloseTicket** and **argSlippage** for the closing order ticket and the slippage, respectively. If the order was not closed successfully, we run the error handling block, which prints the ticket number and current Ask price to the log.

The code to close a sell order will be identical, except that you'd use the Bid price for the **ClosePrice** variable. You can view the sell market close function in Appendix D.

Pending Order Close Function

Here's a function to close a single pending order. This will work on all pending order types, buy and sell.

```
bool ClosePendingOrder(string argSymbol, int argCloseTicket, double argSlippage)
   {
      OrderSelect(argCloseTicket,SELECT_BY_TICKET);

   if(OrderCloseTime() == 0)
      {
         while(IsTradeContextBusy()) Sleep(10);
         bool Deleted = OrderDelete(argCloseTicket,Red);

         if(Deleted == false)
           {
              int ErrorCode = GetLastError();
              string ErrDesc = ErrorDescription(ErrorCode);

              string ErrAlert = StringConcatenate("Close Pending Order -  Error: ",
                ErrorCode,": ",ErrDesc);
              Alert(ErrAlert);

              string ErrLog = StringConcatenate("Ticket: ",argCloseTicket,
                " Bid: ",MarketInfo(argSymbol,MODE_BID),
                " Ask: ",MarketInfo(argSymbol,MODE_ASK));
              Print(ErrLog);
           }
      }
   return(Deleted);
   }
```

Stop Loss & Take Profit Calculation Functions

We're going to create a few short functions for calculating stop loss and take profit as discussed on pages 25-30. We will pass our external variables indicating the stop loss or take profit in pips to our function, as well as the order opening price. The return value of our function will be the actual stop loss or take profit price.

Here's the function to calculate a buy stop loss in pips:

```
double CalcBuyStopLoss(string argSymbol, int argStopLoss, double argOpenPrice)
   {
      if(argStopLoss == 0) return(0);
      double BuyStopLoss = argOpenPrice - (argStopLoss * PipPoint(argSymbol));
      return(BuyStopLoss);
   }
```

First, we'll check to see if a valid stop loss level has been passed along with the function. If the **argStopLoss** argument is 0, then we return a value of 0 to the calling function, indicating that no stop loss was specified.

Next, we calculate the stop loss by subtracting the stop loss in pips from the order opening price. We multiply **argStopLoss** by **PipPoint()** to calculate the fractional value, and subtract that from **argOpenPrice**. We will use either the Bid or Ask price (for market orders) or the intended pending order price.

Note that we do not check the stop level or otherwise verify that the stop loss is valid. We will use another set of functions to verify or adjust the stop loss price as necessary. You could, of course, easily modify this function to verify the stop loss price, display an error message, or automatically adjust the price.

Here is the function to calculate a buy take profit in pips:

```
double CalcBuyTakeProfit(string argSymbol, int argTakeProfit, double argOpenPrice)
   {
     if(argTakeProfit == 0) return(0);
     double BuyTakeProfit = OpenPrice + (argTakeProfit * PipPoint(argSymbol));
     return(BuyTakeProfit);
   }
```

The functions for calculating stop loss and take profit for sell orders are listed in Appendix D. Note that the function for calculating sell stop loss is nearly identical to the one above for calculating the buy take profit, and likewise for buy stop loss and sell take profit.

Stop Level Verification

We're going to create two sets of functions to calculate and verify stop levels. The first will simply calculate the stop level above or below a specified price, and return a boolean value indicating whether the indicated price is inside or outside the stop level. A second set of functions will automatically adjust a price so that it is outside the stop level, plus or minus a specified number of pips.

The following function verifies whether a price is above the upper stop level (the order opening price plus the stop level). If so, the function returns true, otherwise false:

```
bool VerifyUpperStopLevel(string argSymbol, double argVerifyPrice,
   double argOpenPrice = 0)
   {
      double StopLevel = MarketInfo(argSymbol,MODE_STOPLEVEL) * Point;

      if(argOpenPrice == 0) double OpenPrice = MarketInfo(argSymbol,MODE_ASK);
      else OpenPrice = argOpenPrice;

      double UpperStopLevel = OpenPrice + StopLevel;

      if(argVerifyPrice > UpperStopLevel) bool StopVerify = true;
      else StopVerify = false;

      return(StopVerify);
   }
```

We pass the currency symbol, the price to verify, and the order opening price (optional) as arguments. By default, the stop level is calculated relative to the Ask price. If **argOpenPrice** is specified, the stop level will be calculated relative to that price instead. (Use this when verifying stop loss and take profit prices for pending orders).

The function will check to see whether **argVerifyPrice** is greater than the **UpperStopLevel**. If it is, the return value will be true. Otherwise, false. You can use this function to check for a valid stop loss, take profit or pending order price, without modifying the original price. Here's an example where we check a stop loss price and show an error message if the price is not valid:

```
bool Verified = VerifyUpperStopLevel(Symbol(),SellStopLoss);

if(Verified == false) Alert("Sell stop loss is invalid!");
```

The code to check the stop level below the current or pending price is in Appendix D. Our second set of functions is similar, except that they will automatically adjust the invalid stop loss, take profit or pending order price to a valid one:

```
double AdjustAboveStopLevel(string argSymbol, double argAdjustPrice, int argAddPips = 0,
   double argOpenPrice = 0)
   {
      double StopLevel = MarketInfo(argSymbol,MODE_STOPLEVEL) * Point;

      if(argOpenPrice == 0) double OpenPrice = MarketInfo(argSymbol,MODE_ASK);
      else OpenPrice = argOpenPrice;

      double UpperStopLevel = OpenPrice + StopLevel;
```

```
        if(argAdjustPrice <= UpperStopLevel)
          {
            double AdjustedPrice = UpperStopLevel + (argAddPips * PipPoint(argSymbol));
          }
        else AdjustedPrice = argAdjustPrice;

        return(AdjustedPrice);
      }
```

The argument **argAdjustPrice** is the price we will verify and adjust if it's invalid. We've added a new optional parameter, **argAddPips**. This will add the specified number of pips to the stop level price when adjusting an invalid price.

As before, we calculate the stop level, relative to either the Ask price or the **argOpenPrice** parameter. If the **argAdjustPrice** parameter is inside the stop level (*i.e.* not valid), the price will be adjusted so that it is outside the stop level by the number of pips specified by **argAddPips**.

If the price specified by **argAdjustPrice** is valid, that price will be passed back to the calling function. In any case, the return value is the one you will want to use for your take profit, stop loss or pending order price. We will be using these functions in this book to verify stop levels and adjust our prices accordingly. The functions to calculate and verify the lower stop level can be found in Appendix D.

Add Stop Loss and Take Profit

In keeping with our idea to keep functions focused on simple and discrete tasks, we've moved our order modification to a separate function. This function will add or modify the stop loss and take profit on the specified order. We'll assume the stop loss and take profit prices have already been calculated and verified:

```
  bool AddStopProfit(int argTicket, double argStopLoss, double argTakeProfit)
    {
      if(argStopLoss == 0 && argTakeProfit == 0) return(false);

      OrderSelect(argTicket,SELECT_BY_TICKET);
      double OpenPrice = OrderOpenPrice();

      while(IsTradeContextBusy()) Sleep(10);

      // Modify Order
      bool TicketMod = OrderModify(argTicket,OrderOpenPrice(),argStopLoss,argTakeProfit,0);
```

```
        // Error Handling
        if(TicketMod == false)
          {
            int ErrorCode = GetLastError();
            string ErrDesc = ErrorDescription(ErrorCode);

            string ErrAlert = StringConcatenate("Add Stop/Profit - Error ",ErrorCode,": ",
              ErrDesc);
            Alert(ErrAlert);

            string ErrLog = StringConcatenate("Bid: ",MarketInfo(OrderSymbol(),MODE_BID),
              " Ask: ",MarketInfo(OrderSymbol(),MODE_ASK)," Ticket: ",argTicket,
              " Stop: ",argStopLoss," Profit: ",argTakeProfit);
            Print(ErrLog);
          }

      return(TicketMod);
    }
```

We check first to see if either a stop loss or a take profit price has been supplied. If not, we will exit the function. Otherwise, we will modify the order using the stop loss and take profit that was passed to the function. The error handling function will run if the order modification was not successful. This function will work on all order types.

Using Include Files

To keep our functions organized for easy inclusion in our source code files, we'll place the functions into an include file. An include file can consist of function declarations, imported functions, and any global or external variables that you wish to include in an expert advisor.

Include files require no special syntax. You declare the functions and variables in the include file just as you would in any source code file. Include files should not have an **init()**, **start()** or **deinit()** function. The file must have an **.mqh** extension and be located in the **\experts\include** folder.

All of the functions we create in this book will be placed in an include file named **IncludeExample.mqh**. The contents of this file are listed in Appendix D.

Using Libraries

A library is a compiled collection of functions. Whereas an include file is a source code file whose contents are "included" in the executable file, a library is a separate executable that contains the imported functions. Therefore you must have both your expert advisor executable and the library executable to run your EA.

Libraries are stored in the `\experts\libraries` folder. The source code files have an `.mq4` extension, and the executables have an `.ex4` extension. Libraries do not have a `start()`, `init()` or `deinit()` function. To declare a file as a library, you must place the `#property library` preprocessor directive at the beginning of the file.

The advantage of libraries is that they are compiled, so if you need to distribute a function library, you can do so without exposing your intellectual property as you would if you distributed an include file. You can also make bug fixes to a library without having to recompile your expert advisors – as long as you do not make any changes to the function declarations, such as adding and removing arguments or functions.

There are a few disadvantages to libraries as well. Since they are already compiled, it is not possible for the compiler to check if the parameters are correct. You cannot specify a default value for a parameter in a library function, which means you will need to specify a value for every argument in a function call. You cannot use external variables in a library, or create globally scoped variables that your expert advisor can access.

You'll need to use the `#import` directive to import library functions into your expert advisor. If the library contains numerous functions, it may be best to create an include file with the `#import` statements. This increases the number of files you'll need to work with. Unless you have a very good reason to use libraries, it is suggested that you stick with include files for storing your functions.

You can also import functions from Windows DLLs using `#import` directives. The `WinUser32.mqh` include file in `\experts\includes` has numerous examples that are used for the `MessageBox()` function. (We'll discuss the `MessageBox()` function in chapter 8). Using DLL functions is an advanced usage that we will not cover here. There are articles on the MQL4 website on using DLLs for those who are interested.

A Simple Expert Advisor (with Functions)

Here is our expert advisor source code, as it appears in the source code file. We'll assume that the functions we've created in this chapter are declared in the include file **IncludeExample.mqh**, the contents of which are listed in Appendix D.

```
// Preprocessor
#include <IncludeExample.mqh>


// External Variables
extern bool DynamicLotSize = true;
extern double EquityPercent = 2;
extern double FixedLotSize = 0.1;
```

```
extern double StopLoss = 50;
extern double TakeProfit = 100;

extern int Slippage = 5;
extern int MagicNumber = 123;

extern int FastMAPeriod = 10;
extern int SlowMAPeriod = 20;


// Global Variables
int BuyTicket;
int SellTicket;
double UsePoint;
int UseSlippage;


// Init function
int init()
  {
    UsePoint = PipPoint(Symbol());
    UseSlippage = GetSlippage(Symbol(),Slippage);
  }


// Start Function
int start()
  {
    // Moving Average
    double FastMA = iMA(NULL,0,FastMAPeriod,0,0,0,0);
    double SlowMA = iMA(NULL,0,SlowMAPeriod,0,0,0,0);

    // Calculate Lot Size
    double LotSize = CalcLotSize(DynamicLotSize,EquityPercent,StopLoss,FixedLotSize);
    LotSize = VerifyLotSize(LotSize);

    // Buy Order
    if(FastMA > SlowMA && BuyTicket == 0)
      {
        if(SellTicket > 0) int Closed = CloseSellOrder(Symbol(),SellTicket,UseSlippage);
        SellTicket = 0;

        BuyTicket = OpenBuyOrder(Symbol(),LotSize,UseSlippage,MagicNumber);

        if(BuyTicket > 0 && (StopLoss > 0 || TakeProfit > 0))
          {
            OrderSelect(BuyTicket,SELECT_BY_TICKET);
            double OpenPrice = OrderOpenPrice();
```

```
            double BuyStopLoss = CalcBuyStopLoss(Symbol(),StopLoss,OpenPrice);
            if(BuyStopLoss > 0)
               {
                  BuyStopLoss = AdjustBelowStopLevel(Symbol(),BuyStopLoss,5);
               }

            double BuyTakeProfit = CalcBuyTakeProfit(Symbol(),TakeProfit,OpenPrice);
            if(BuyTakeProfit > 0)
               {
                  BuyTakeProfit = AdjustAboveStopLevel(Symbol(),BuyTakeProfit,5);
               }

            AddStopProfit(BuyTicket,BuyStopLoss,BuyTakeProfit);
         }
      }


   // Sell Order
   if(FastMA < SlowMA && SellTicket == 0)
      {
         if(BuyTicket > 0) Closed = CloseBuyOrder(Symbol(),BuyTicket,Slippage);
         BuyTicket = 0;

         SellTicket = OpenSellOrder(Symbol(),LotSize,UseSlippage,MagicNumber);

         if(SellTicket > 0 && (StopLoss > 0 || TakeProfit > 0))
            {
               OrderSelect(SellTicket,SELECT_BY_TICKET);
               OpenPrice = OrderOpenPrice();

               double SellStopLoss = CalcSellStopLoss(Symbol(),StopLoss,OpenPrice);
               if(SellStopLoss > 0)
                  {
                     SellStopLoss = AdjustAboveStopLevel(Symbol(),SellStopLoss,5);
                  }

               double SellTakeProfit = CalcSellTakeProfit(Symbol(),TakeProfit,OpenPrice);
               if(SellTakeProfit > 0)
                  {
                     SellTakeProfit = AdjustBelowStopLevel(Symbol(),SellTakeProfit,5);
                  }

               AddStopProfit(SellTicket,SellStopLoss,SellTakeProfit);
            }
      }
   return(0);
}
```

We begin by including the file that has our functions in it, in this case **IncludeExample.mqh**. The variable declarations and the contents of the **init()** function are the same as before. At the beginning of the **start()** function, we use **CalcLotSize()** and **VerifyLotSize()** to to calculate and verify our lot size.

In our buy and sell order blocks, we use **CloseBuyOrder()** and **CloseSellOrder()** to close the opposite order. Our new orders are opened using **OpenBuyOrder()** or **OpenSellOrder()**. Before calculating the stop loss and take profit, we check that the order was opened and that a **StopLoss** or **TakeProfit** has been specified.

We retrieving the opening price of the order using **OrderSelect()** and **OrderOpenPrice()**. We then calculate our stop loss using **CalcBuyStopLoss()** or **CalcSellStopLoss()**, and our take profit using **CalcBuyTakeProfit()** or **CalcSellTakeProfit()**.

We check to see if the stop loss or take profit is greater than 0, and use the functions **AdjustAboveStopLevel()** and **AdjustBelowStopLevel()** to verify our stop loss and take profit prices. Finally, we pass those prices to the **AddOrderProfit()** function, which adds the stop loss and take profit to the order.

The EA above does exactly the same thing as the code starting on page 51, but is much easier to read. By breaking the code into functions, we have de-cluttered our source code and made our EA easier to manage. We will add a few more features to this expert advisor before the end of the book. You can view the complete code in Appendix C.

The initial work in creating these functions will take some time, but it will save you time in the long run, as you will more easily be able to prototype trading ideas and turn out working expert advisors in a short amount of time.

Chapter 5
Order Management

You've already been introduced to the **OrderSelect()** function in chapter 2. In this section, we will use the **OrderSelect()** function, along with the cycle operators **for** and **while**, to loop through the order pool and retrieve order information. This method will be used to close multiple orders, add trailing stops, count the number of open orders, and more.

The Order Loop

The `for` Operator

The **for** operator is used to loop through a block of code a predetermined number of times. We declare an integer variable to use as a counter, and assign it a starting value. We indicate the condition which, if true, will cause the loop to run. We also indicate an expression by which to increment the counter variable.

Here is an example of a **for** loop:

```
for(int Counter = 1; Counter <= 3; Counter++)
   {
     // Code to loop
   }
```

The first expression, **int Counter = 1**, initializes our **Counter** variable with a value of 1. The second expression, **Counter <= 3**, is the condition which, if true, will execute the code inside the braces. If false, the loop is ended, and execution continues after the end brace (**}**).

The third expression, **Counter++**, means "increment the value of **Counter** by one." The expression **Counter--** would decrement the value by one, and **Counter+2** would increment by two. Every time the loop completes, the counter variable is incremented or decremented. On the next iteration of the loop, the second argument, in this case **Counter<= 3**, is re-evaluated. Note that there is no semicolon after the third expression.

The above example will execute the loop three times. After each iteration, the counter is incremented by one, and after the third iteration the loop will terminate.

The `while` Operator

The `while` operator is a simpler method of looping in MQL. The `for` loop is best if you know exactly how many times you plan on executing the loop. If you're unsure of the number of iterations however, then the `while` loop would be more appropriate.

Here's an example of a `while` loop:

```
while(Something == true)
   {
      // Loop code
   }
```

This literal example uses a boolean variable called **Something**. If **Something** is equal to **true**, the loop will execute. Of course, if the value of **Something** never changes, the loop will run endlessly. Thus, it is necessary that there be a condition to change the value of **Something** at some point during the loop. Once this condition is true, **Something** is changed to **false**, and the loop will stop executing.

You could also increment a variable, just like you would using the `for` operator:

```
int Counter = 1;
while(Counter <= 3)
   {
      Counter++;
   }
```

This code will execute exactly like the `for` loop above!

The Order Loop

Here is the code we will use to loop through the pool of open orders:

```
for(Counter = 0; Counter <= OrdersTotal()-1; Counter++)
   {
      OrderSelect(Counter,SELECT_BY_POS);
      // Evaluate condition
   }
```

We will set the value of **Counter** to 0, and iterate the loop as long as **Counter** is less than or equal to the value of **OrdersTotal()**, minus one. **Counter** will be incremented by 1 after each iteration of the loop.

OrdersTotal() is a function that returns the number of currently opened orders. Why are we subtracting 1 from the value of **OrdersTotal()**? Let's explain how the order pool works:

The order pool contains all orders that are currently open in our terminal, including manually placed orders as well as orders placed by expert advisors. The order indexes are numbered starting from zero. If there is one order open, its index is 0. When a second order is opened, its index is 1. If a third order is opened, its index will be 2, and so on. Index 0 is the oldest order, and index 2 is the newest.

OrdersTotal() will return the number of currently opened orders. In the above example, we have three orders open. But because our order index starts at 0, we want our counter variable to only count to 2. The value of **Counter** must correspond with our order index numbers, so that is why we must subtract 1 from **OrdersTotal()**.

When an order in the open order pool is closed, any newer orders in the pool will have their order indexes decremented. For example if the order with index 0 is closed, then the order with index 1 becomes index 0, and order index 2 becomes index 1. This is important when we close orders, and we'll cover this in more detail soon.

Back to our order loop: The **OrderSelect()** statement uses our **Counter** variable as the order position index. As explained above, we will increment our way through the order pool from the oldest order to the newest. The **SELECT_BY_POS** parameter indicates that we are selecting the order by its position in the order pool, as opposed to its ticket number.

For the first iteration of this loop, **Counter** will be equal to 0 and we will select the oldest order from the order pool using **OrderSelect()**. We can then examine the order information using functions such as **OrderTicket()** or **OrderStopLoss()**, and modify or close the order as necessary.

Order Counting

It is often very useful to find out how many orders our EA has open, and of what type. We will create several order counting functions to count the current number of open orders, based on the order type. The following function will count the total number of open orders:

```
int TotalOrderCount(string argSymbol, int argMagicNumber)
  {
    int OrderCount;
    for(Counter = 0; Counter <= OrdersTotal()-1; Counter++)
      {
        OrderSelect(Counter,SELECT_BY_POS);
```

```
      if(OrderMagicNumber() == argMagicNumber && OrderSymbol() == argSymbol)
        {
          OrderCount++;
        }
    }
  return(OrderCount);
}
```

We've named our order counting function **TotalOrderCount()**. It will return an integer value indicating how many orders are currently opened on the specified chart symbol matching the magic number that we've passed as a function argument.

We start by declaring the **OrderCount** variable. Since we have not indicated an initial value, **OrderCount** will be initialized as 0. You'll recognize the **for** operator and the **OrderSelect()** function from the previous section.

Since the order pool contains all open orders, including those placed by other EAs, it is necessary for us to identify which orders were placed by our EA. We check the **OrderSymbol()** of the selected order first, and make sure that it matches the **argSymbol** argument. The we check the magic number on the order.

If **OrderMagicNumber()** matches the **argMagicNumber** argument, we can be fairly sure that this order was placed by this EA. As long as the user is not running two EA's on the same currency symbol with the same magic number, we can be certain that this order was placed by this EA. When running multiple expert advisors on the same instrument, take care to ensure that you're using a unique magic number on each EA.

If the order matches both our magic number and our chart symbol, the value of **OrderCount** will be incremented by one. After we have looped through all of the orders in the order pool, we return the value of **OrderCount** to the calling function.

Here's an example of how we would use this in code:

```
if(TotalOrderCount(Symbol(),MagicNumber) > 0 && CloseOrders == true)
  {
    // Close all orders
  }
```

If there are orders opened by this EA, and the value of **CloseOrders** is **true** (we'll assume this was set somewhere else in the program), then the code inside the braces will run, which will close all open orders.

Let's modify our order counting routine to count only buy market orders:

```
int BuyMarketCount(string argSymbol, int argMagicNumber)
  {
    int OrderCount;
    for(Counter = 0; Counter <= OrdersTotal()-1; Counter++)
      {
        OrderSelect(Counter,SELECT_BY_POS);
        if(OrderMagicNumber() == argMagicNumber && OrderSymbol() == argSymbol
           && OrderType() == OP_BUY)
          {
            OrderCount++;
          }
      }
    return(OrderCount);
  }
```

The code is identical to before, except that we've added the **OrderType()** function to check the order type of the currently selected order. **OP_BUY** is the constant that indicates a buy market order. To count other types of orders, simply replace **OP_BUY** with the appropriate order type constant, and rename the function to reflect the order type.

It is suggested that you create an order counting function for every order type. You can view the code for all of the order counting functions in Appendix D.

Closing Multiple Orders

More often that not, we'll need to close multiple orders of the same type. We'll combine our order loop with our order closing routines to close multiple orders at once. This function will close all buy market orders placed by our expert advisor:

```
void CloseAllBuyOrders(string argSymbol, int argMagicNumber, int argSlippage)
  {
    for(int Counter = 0; Counter <= OrdersTotal()-1; Counter++)
      {
        OrderSelect(Counter,SELECT_BY_POS);

        if(OrderMagicNumber() == argMagicNumber && OrderSymbol() == argSymbol
           && OrderType() == OP_BUY)
          {
            // Close Order
            int CloseTicket = OrderTicket();
            double CloseLots = OrderLots();

            while(IsTradeContextBusy()) Sleep(10);
            double ClosePrice = MarketInfo(argSymbol,MODE_BID);
```

```
        bool Closed = OrderClose(CloseTicket,CloseLots,ClosePrice,argSlippage,Red);

        // Error Handling
        if(Closed == false)
          {
            ErrorCode = GetLastError();
            string ErrDesc = ErrorDescription(ErrorCode);

            string ErrAlert = StringConcatenate("Close All Buy Orders - Error ",
              ErrorCode,": ",ErrDesc);
            Alert(ErrAlert);

            string ErrLog = StringConcatenate("Bid: ",
              MarketInfo(argSymbol,MODE_BID)," Ticket: ",CloseTicket,
              " Price: ",ClosePrice);
            Print(ErrLog);
          }
        else Counter--;
      }
    }
  }
```

Note that we are using **void** as the function data type. We've determined that there is no useful data to return from this function, so we are not requiring a **return** operator in the function.

You'll recognize the **for** loop and the **OrderSelect()** function from our order loop code. We will loop through the order pool and examine each order to see if we need to close it. If the current order is a buy market order, as indicated by **OP_BUY**, and if it matches our chart symbol and magic number arguments, we'll proceed to close the order.

We call the **OrderTicket()** function to retrieve the ticket number for the current order. From here, our code is identical to the buy market close code in previous chapters. Note the very last statement: **Counter--**. If the order was closed properly, the **Counter** variable will be decremented by one.

We explained earlier that when an order is closed, all of the orders behind it have their indexes decremented by one. If we did not decrement the counter variable after closing an order, subsequent orders would be skipped.

There's a very good reason why we loop through the orders from oldest to newest: The NFA regulations that went into effect in summer 2009 for US brokers requires that multiple orders placed on the same currency symbol be closed in the order that they were placed. This is called the FIFO (first in, first out) rule. Looping through the orders from oldest to newest ensures that we comply with the FIFO rule when closing orders.

To close sell market orders using the above code, simply change the order type to **OP_SELL** and the **ClosePrice** to the symbol's Ask price. The sell order close function can be viewed in Appendix D.

Let's examine the code to close multiple pending orders. This example will close all buy stop orders. The difference between this code and the code to close buy market orders above is that we specify **OP_BUYSTOP** as our order type, and we use **OrderDelete()** to close the orders.

```
void CloseAllBuyStopOrders(string argSymbol, int argMagicNumber, int argSlippage)
  {
    for(int Counter = 0; Counter <= OrdersTotal()-1; Counter++)
      {
        OrderSelect(Counter,SELECT_BY_POS);

        if(OrderMagicNumber() == argMagicNumber && OrderSymbol() == argSymbol
          && OrderType() == OP_BUYSTOP)
          {
            // Delete Order
            int CloseTicket = OrderTicket();

            while(IsTradeContextBusy()) Sleep(10);

            bool Closed = OrderDelete(CloseTicket,Red);

            // Error Handling
            if(Closed == false)
              {
                ErrorCode = GetLastError();
                string ErrDesc = ErrorDescription(ErrorCode);

                string ErrAlert = StringConcatenate("Close All Buy Stop Orders",
                  " - Error ",ErrorCode,": ",ErrDesc);
                Alert(ErrAlert);

                string ErrLog = StringConcatenate("Bid: ",
                  MarketInfo(argSymbol,MODE_BID)," Ask: ",
                  MarketInfo(argSymbol,MODE_ASK)," Ticket: ",CloseTicket);
                Print(ErrLog);
              }
            else Counter--;
          }
      }
  }
```

This code will work for all types of pending orders – simply change the order type comparison to the type of order you wish to close. The order closing functions for all pending orders can be viewed in Appendix D.

Trailing Stops

We can also use our order loop to modify multiple orders. A common example of this is the trailing stop. A trailing stop moves the stop loss up or down with the order price as the order gains in profit. This "locks in" profit and provides excellent loss protection.

The trailing stop is expressed as a maximum number of pips. For example, if your trailing stop is 50 pips, the stop loss will never be more than 50 pips away from your price. If the price reverses and the profit declines, the stop loss will stay where it is. The stop only moves in the direction of profit – never in reverse.

When modifying a trailing stop, we must check to see if the distance in pips between the current price and the current stop loss is greater that the trailing stop. If so, the stop loss will be modified so that the distance from the current price in pips is equal to the number of pips in the trailing stop setting.

The trailing stop is calculated relative to the closing price, which is the Bid for buy orders, and the Ask for sell orders. Note that this is the opposite of the opening price. Let's examine the code for modifying a trailing stop. First, we declare the external variable for our trailing stop setting:

```
extern double TrailingStop = 50;
```

This code checks all buy market orders and modifies the stop loss as necessary:

```
for(int Counter = 0; Counter <= OrdersTotal()-1; Counter++)
  {
    OrderSelect(Counter,SELECT_BY_POS);

    double MaxStopLoss = MarketInfo(Symbol(),MODE_BID) -
      (TrailingStop * PipPoint(Symbol()));

    MaxStopLoss = NormalizeDouble(MaxStopLoss,MarketInfo(OrderSymbol(),MODE_DIGITS));

    double CurrentStop = NormalizeDouble(OrderStopLoss(),
      MarketInfo(OrderSymbol(),MODE_DIGITS));

    // Modify Stop
    if(OrderMagicNumber() == MagicNumber && OrderSymbol() == Symbol()
      && OrderType() == OP_BUY && CurrentStop < MaxStopLoss)
      {
        bool Trailed = OrderModify(OrderTicket(),OrderOpenPrice(),MaxStopLoss,
          OrderTakeProfit(),0);
```

```
                // Error Handling
                if(Trailed == false)
                  {
                     ErrorCode = GetLastError();
                     string ErrDesc = ErrorDescription(ErrorCode);

                     string ErrAlert = StringConcatenate("Buy Trailing Stop -  Error ",
                        ErrorCode,": ",ErrDesc);
                     Alert(ErrAlert);

                     string ErrLog = StringConcatenate("Bid: "MarketInfo(Symbol(),MODE_BID),
                        " Ticket: ",CloseTicket," Stop: ",OrderStopLoss()," Trail: ",
                        MaxStopLoss);
                     Print(ErrLog);
                  }
              }
          }
```

After selecting the order from the pool with **OrderSelect()**, we determine the maximum stop loss distance by subtracting our trailing stop setting, multiplied by **PipPoint()**, from the current Bid price. This is stored in the variable **MaxStopLoss**.

We use the MQL function **NormalizeDouble()** to round the **MaxStopLoss** variable to the correct number of digits after the decimal point. Prices in MetaTrader can be quoted up to eight decimal places. By using **NormalizeDouble()**, we round that down to 4 or 5 digits (2-3 digits for JPY pairs).

Next, we retrieve the stop loss of the currently selected order, and round it using **NormalizeDouble()** just to be sure. We assign this value to the variable **CurrentStop**.

Then we check to see if the current order needs to be modified. If magic number, symbol and order type match, and the current stop loss (**CurrentStop**) is less than **MaxStopLoss**, then we modify the order's stop loss. We pass the **MaxStopLoss** variable as our new stop loss to the **OrderModify()** function.

If the **OrderModify()** function was not successful, the error handling routine will run, and the current price information, ticket number, current stop loss and modified stop loss will be printed to the log.

The trailing stop conditions for sell orders are different, and need to be addressed separately. Here are the conditions to modify a sell order:

```
    // Modify Stop
    if(OrderMagicNumber() == MagicNumber && OrderSymbol() == Symbol()
       && OrderType() == OP_SELL && (CurrentStop > MaxStopLoss || CurrentStop == 0))
```

Note the condition (`CurrentStop > MaxStopLoss || CurrentStop == 0`). If there is no stop loss placed with the order, then the condition `CurrentStop > MaxStopLoss` will never be true, because `MaxStopLoss` will never be less than zero. Thus, we add an OR condition, `CurrentStop == 0`.

If the current order's stop loss is 0 (no stop loss), then as long as the remaining conditions are true, the trailing stop will be placed.

Minimum Profit

Let's enhance our trailing stop by adding a minimum profit level. In the above example, the trailing stop will kick in right away. If you set an initial stop loss of 100 pips, and your trailing stop is 50 pips, the stop loss would be set to 50 pips immediately, invalidating your initial 100 pip stop loss.

Adding a minimum profit level will allow you to set an initial stop loss, while delaying the trailing stop until a specified amount of profit is reached. In this example, let's assume an initial stop loss of 100 pips is set when the order is placed. We're using a trailing stop of 50 pips, with a minimum profit level of 50 pips. When the profit for the order reaches 50 pips, the stop loss will be adjusted to break even.

Let's add an external variable for our minimum profit setting:

```
extern int TrailingStop = 50;
extern int MinimumProfit = 50;
```

The following function modifies the stop loss for all buy market orders, checking the minimum profit before doing so:

```
void BuyTrailingStop(string argSymbol, int argTrailingStop, int argMinProfit,
  int argMagicNumber)
  {
    for(int Counter = 0; Counter <= OrdersTotal()-1; Counter++)
      {
        OrderSelect(Counter,SELECT_BY_POS);

        // Calculate Max Stop and Min Profit
        double MaxStopLoss = MarketInfo(argSymbol,MODE_BID) -
          (TrailingStop * PipPoint(argSymbol));

        MaxStopLoss = NormalizeDouble(MaxStopLoss,
          MarketInfo(OrderSymbol(),MODE_DIGITS));

        double CurrentStop = NormalizeDouble(OrderStopLoss(),
          MarketInfo(OrderSymbol(),MODE_DIGITS));
```

```
          double PipsProfit = MarketInfo(argSymbol,MODE_BID) - OrderOpenPrice();
          double MinProfit = MinimumProfit * PipPoint(argSymbol));

          // Modify Stop
          if(OrderMagicNumber() == argMagicNumber && OrderSymbol() == argSymbol
             && OrderType() == OP_BUY && CurrentStop < MaxStopLoss
             && PipsProfit >= MinProfit)
             {
               bool Trailed = OrderModify(OrderTicket(),OrderOpenPrice(),MaxStopLoss,
                 OrderTakeProfit(),0);

               // Error Handling
               if(Trailed == false)
                 {
                   ErrorCode = GetLastError();
                   string ErrDesc = ErrorDescription(ErrorCode);

                   string ErrAlert = StringConcatenate("Buy Trailing Stop - Error ",
                     ErrorCode,": ",ErrDesc);
                   Alert(ErrAlert);

                   string ErrLog = StringConcatenate("Bid: ",
                     MarketInfo(argSymbol,MODE_BID)," Ticket: ",CloseTicket,
                     " Stop: ",OrderStopLoss()," Trail: ",MaxStopLoss);
                   Print(ErrLog);
                 }
             }
        }
     }
```

We calculate the current order profit in pips by subtracting **OrderOpenPrice()** from the current Bid price, and storing that in the variable **PipsProfit**. We compare that to our minimum profit setting, which is multiplied by **PipPoint()** and stored in the variable **MinProfit**.

If the current profit in pips (**PipsProfit**) is greater than or equal to our minimum profit (**MinProfit**), and all of the other conditions are true, the stop will be modified.

The trailing stop with the minimum profit setting is much more flexible, so you'll probably want to use this function in your expert advisor. See Appendix D for the complete sell trailing stop code.

Break Even Stop

You can also use this method to apply a break even stop adjustment to your orders. A break even stop adjusts the stop loss to be equal to the order opening price, after a certain level of profit has been reached. The break even stop is independent from your initial stop loss and trailing stop functions.

Here is the external variable for our break even profit setting. The minimum profit is specified in pips.

```
extern double BreakEvenProfit = 25;
```

This code will modify the stop loss on all buy market orders to break even, once the order profit in pips is equal to or greater than **BreakEvenProfit**. We will not be creating a function for this, but you can do so if you feel it would be useful.

```
for(int Counter = 0; Counter <= OrdersTotal()-1; Counter++)
  {
    OrderSelect(Counter,SELECT_BY_POS);
    RefreshRates();

    double PipsProfit = Bid - OrderOpenPrice();
    double MinProfit = BreakEvenProfit * PipPoint(OrderSymbol()));

    if(OrderMagicNumber() == MagicNumber && OrderSymbol() == Symbol()
      && OrderType() == OP_BUY && PipsProfit >= MinProfit
      && OrderOpenPrice() != OrderStopLoss())
      {
        bool BreakEven = OrderModify(OrderTicket(),OrderOpenPrice(),
          OrderOpenPrice(),OrderTakeProfit(),0);

        if(BreakEven == false)
          {
            ErrorCode = GetLastError();
            string ErrDesc = ErrorDescription(ErrorCode);

            string ErrAlert = StringConcatenate("Buy Break Even - Error ",
              ErrorCode,": ",ErrDesc);
            Alert(ErrAlert);

            string ErrLog = StringConcatenate("Bid: ",Bid,", Ask: ",Ask,
              ", Ticket: ",CloseTicket,", Stop: ",OrderStopLoss(),", Break: ",
              MinProfit);
            Print(ErrLog);
          }
      }
  }
```

We subtract the order opening price from the current Bid price to calculate the current profit in pips, and store this in **PipsProfit**. We calculate the minimum profit in pips and store that in **MinProfit**. If **PipsProfit** is greater than or equal to **MinProfit**, then we will modify the stop loss to be equal to the order opening price.

We also check to make sure that the stop loss is not already set at the break even price. If **OrderOpenPrice()** is not equal to **OrderStopLoss()**, then we can proceed.

Updating the Expert Advisor

Let's modify the **start()** function of our moving average cross expert advisor to reflect the new functions we have created. First, we will check to see if there are any buy orders open before we open more. Instead of closing a single sell order, we will simply use the function to close all sell orders. This method does not require us to use an order ticket.

```
// Buy Order
if(FastMA > SlowMA && BuyTicket == 0 && BuyMarketCount(Symbol(),MagicNumber) == 0)
  {
    if(SellMarketCount(Symbol(),MagicNumber) > 0)
      {
        CloseAllSellOrders(Symbol(),MagicNumber,Slippage);
      }

    SellTicket = 0;

    BuyTicket = OpenBuyOrder(Symbol(),LotSize,UseSlippage,MagicNumber);
  }
```

We used the function **BuyMarketCount()** that we defined on page 84 to return the number of buy orders currently open. We will keep the **BuyTicket** check in, so that only alternating buy/sell orders are opened.

The function **CloseAllSellOrders()** closes any sell orders that are open. We check **SellMarketCount()** first to see if there are any sell orders to close. This function does not require an order ticket, unlike the **CloseSellOrder()** function in chapter 4. It is recommended you use this method for closing out opposite orders in your EA, as it is more robust.

The rest of the buy order placement code is the same as before. The corresponding sell order placement code is below:

```
// Sell Order
if(FastMA < SlowMA && SellTicket == 0 && SellMarketCount(Symbol(),MagicNumber) == 0)
  {
    if(BuyMarketCount(Symbol(),MagicNumber) > 0)
      {
        CloseAllBuyOrders(Symbol(),MagicNumber,Slippage);
      }

    BuyTicket = 0;

    SellTicket = OpenSellOrder(Symbol(),LotSize,UseSlippage,MagicNumber);
  }
```

Next, let's add the trailing stop functions to our order. We'll perform the trailing stop routine after our order placement. As above, we will check for open buy or sell orders before calling the trailing stop function. Let's add the following external variables to our EA:

```
extern int TrailingStop = 50;
extern int MinimumProfit = 50;
```

This is the code to check and modify the trailing stops. Note that we check to see if there is an entry for the **TrailingStop** setting. If it's set to 0, it is effectively disabled:

```
if(BuyMarketCount(Symbol(),MagicNumber) > 0 && TrailingStop > 0)
   {
     BuyTrailingStop(Symbol(),TrailingStop,MinimumProfit,MagicNumber);
   }

if(SellMarketCount(Symbol(),MagicNumber) > 0 && TrailingStop > 0)
   {
     SellTrailingStop(Symbol(),TrailingStop,MinimumProfit,MagicNumber);
   }
```

You can view these changes in context in Appendix C.

Chapter 6
Order Conditions and Indicators

We've spent the last few chapters creating functions that carry out the order mechanics that are common to every expert advisor. These functions are meant to be used in a variety of trading situations, and should be as reusable and flexible as possible. This allows us to concentrate on coding the unique trading conditions for our trading system.

This is where most of your work is going to be focused – getting the expert advisor to trade your system as accurately as possible. We'll need to identify the exact conditions for opening and closing orders, as well as determining stop loss and take profit prices. Almost every trading system uses price and/or indicator data. Let's examine the ways we can access and use this information in our expert advisors.

Price Data

Along with the current Bid or Ask price (which we've already covered in previous chapters), you may need to use bar price data, namely the *high*, *low*, *open* or *close* of a particular bar. For the current chart, you can use the predefined series arrays **High[]**, **Low[]**, **Open[]** and **Close[]**.

An array is a variable that holds multiple values. You cycle through the values by changing the index, which is contained in the square brackets. For example **Open[0]** is the open price of the current bar. 0 is the index, and by changing it, we can get the open price of other bars. The bar previous to the current bar would have an index of 1, and so on. We will frequently be using either the current bar or the previous bar's price values.

If you need a high, low, open or close value for a symbol other than the current chart, or if you need price data for a period other than the current chart period, you can use the functions **iHigh()**, **iLow()**, **iOpen()** and **iClose()**. Here's the syntax of these functions, using **iClose()** as our example:

```
double iClose(string Symbol, int Period, int Shift)
```

- **Symbol** – The symbol of the currency pair to use.

- **Period** – The period of the chart to use, in minutes.

- **Shift** – The backward shift relative to the current bar.

Let's use `iClose()` to get a close price for a different chart period. For example, we're using a 1 hour chart, but we want to check the close price of the previous bar on the 4 hour chart:

```
double H4Close = iClose(NULL,PERIOD_H4,1);
```

`NULL` refers to the current chart symbol. `PERIOD_H4` is an integer constant that refers to the H4 chart period. `1` is our shift, which is the bar previous to the current bar. Let's use another example that returns the close of the current bar on another chart:

```
double GBPClose = iClose(GBPUSD,0,0);
```

`GBPUSD` is the symbol that we're using. We've specified `0` as our period, so the chart period we're checking on `GBPUSD` will be the same as our current chart. The shift is `0`, which is the current bar.

You can use a loop operator such as `for` or `while` to increment the `Shift` parameter and cycle through the chart history. This `for` loop retrieves the close price for each of the last ten bars, and prints it to the log:

```
for(int Count = 0; Count <= 9; Count++)
   {
      double CloseShift = iClose(NULL,0,Count);
      Print(Count+" "+CloseShift);
   }
```

Indicators

The majority of trading systems use indicators to determine trading signals. MetaTrader includes over 20 common indicators, including moving average, MACD, RSI and stochastics. MQL has built-in functions for the stock indicators. You can also use custom indicators in your expert advisor.

Trend Indicators

Let's take a look at the indicator we've been using throughout this book: the moving average. The moving average is a *trend* indicator. It shows whether the price has moved up or down over the indicator period. The moving average consists of a single line drawn on the chart that shows the average price over the last *x* number of bars.

Here is the syntax for the moving average function:

```
double iMA(string Symbol, int Timeframe, int MAPeriod, int MAShift, int MAMethod,
    int MAPrice, int Shift)
```

- **Symbol** – The symbol of the chart to apply the moving average to.

- **Timeframe** – The time period of the chart to apply the moving average to.

Every indicator function in MQL starts off with these two parameters. After this are the indicator-specific parameters. These correspond to the contents of the *Parameters* tab in the *Indicator properties*.

- **MAPeriod** – The look-back period of the moving average.

Almost every indicator has at least one period parameter. Most indicators are calculated using a price series taken from the previous bars. For example, a period setting of 10 would mean that the indicator uses price data from the last ten bars to calculate the indicator value.

- **MAShift** – The forward shift of the moving average line, in bars. This is different than the `Shift` parameter below.

- **MAMethod** – The calculation method of the moving average. Choices include simple, exponential, smoothed or linear weighted.

Any indicator that uses a moving average may give you the option to choose the MA calculation method. We'll talk about moving average methods later in the chapter.

- **MAPrice** – The price array to use when calculating the moving average.

This can be the close, open, high, low or some type of average; such as median, typical or weighted prices. We'll discuss applied price constants later in the chapter.

- **Shift** – The backward shift of the bar to return the calculation for.

The `Shift` parameter is the final parameter in any indicator function. This is the index of the bar to return the indicator value for. A value of 0 returns the indicator value for the current bar. A value of 3 will return the indicator value from 3 bars ago.

The moving average and similar indicators are drawn directly on the chart. You can create trade conditions based on the relationship between indicators and price. Our moving average cross is an example of a price relationship between two indicators. When one indicator's price is greater than the other, a buy or sell signal is generated.

You could also generate trade signals when the current price passes above or below an indicator line. For example, the Bollinger Bands indicator can be used to generate trading signals based on the location of the price in comparison to the upper and lower bands.

Oscillators

The other major type of indicator is an *oscillator*. Oscillators are drawn in a separate window, and as their name suggests, they oscillate between high and low price extremes. Oscillators are either centered around a neutral axis (generally 0), or they are bound by an upper or lower extreme (such as 0 and 100). Examples of oscillators include momentum, stochastics and RSI.

Oscillators indicate *overbought* and *oversold* levels. While they can be used as an indicator of trend, they are generally used to locate areas of pending reversal. These are used to produce *counter-trend* trading signals.

Let's look at a popular oscillator, the *stochastic*. Stochastics consists of two lines, the stochastic line (also called the %K line), and the signal line (the %D line). The stochastic oscillates between 0 and 100. When the stochastic is above 70, it is said to be overbought, and pending a possible reversal. If it is below 30, it is said to be oversold.

Here is the syntax for the stochastic indicator:

```
double iStochastic(string Symbol, int Timeframe, int KPeriod, int Dperiod, int Slowing,
    int MAMethod, int PriceField, int Mode, int Shift)
```

We're already familiar with the first two parameters, **Symbol** and **Timeframe**. Let's examine the indicator-specific parameters:

- **KPeriod** – The period for the %K line.

- **DPeriod** – The period for the %D line.

- **Slowing** – The slowing value for the stochastic. A lower value indicates a fast stochastic, while a higher value indicates a slower one.

- **MAMethod** – The %D line has a moving average method applied to it. This is the same setting as for the moving average. We'll review the moving average methods shortly.

- **PriceField** – Determines the price data used for the %K line. This is either *0: Low/High* or *1: Close/Close*. A value of 1 makes it more likely that the stochastic will trade at it's extremes.

- **Mode** – Determines the stochastic line to calculate – *1: %K line*, or *2: %D line.*

Let's take a moment to talk about the **Mode** parameter. Some indicators draw multiple lines on the chart. The stochastic has two. We will need to call the **iStochastic()** function for both the %K and %D lines, as shown below:

```
double KLine = iStochastic(NULL,0,KPeriod,DPeriod,Slowing,MAMethod,Price,0,0);
double DLine = iStochastic(NULL,0,KPeriod,DPeriod,Slowing,MAMethod,Price,1,0);
```

Note that the **Mode** parameter is 0 for the %K line, and 1 for the %D line. The MQL Reference topic, *Standard Constants – Indicator lines* lists the valid integer constants for the various indicators that use the **Mode** parameter.

You can generate trade signals based on the relationship between the indicator lines and certain indicator levels, such as the overbought and oversold levels of 70 and 30, respectively. You can also evaluate trade signals based on the indicator lines' relationship to each other. For example, you may want to open a buy order only when the %K line is above the %D line. Here are some example conditions:

```
if(KLine < 70) // Buy if stochastic is not overbought
if(KLine > DLine) // Buy if %K is greater than %D
```

The built-in indicator functions are in the MQL Reference under *Technical indicators*. If you'd like more information on an indicator's usage or method of calculation, consult the technical analysis section of the MQL website at **http://ta.mql4.com/**.

Custom Indicators

Hundreds of custom indicators for MetaTrader are available online. If you decide to use a custom indicator in your expert advisor, a little legwork will have to be done. It is best if you have the **.mq4** source code file when using a custom indicator. While it is possible to use a custom indicator without it, having the source code will make it easier to figure out the buffer indexes for the **Mode** parameter.

MQL has a built-in function for handling custom indicators – **iCustom()**. Here is the syntax:

```
double iCustom(string Symbol, int Timeframe, string IndicatorName, Indicator Parameters,
    int Mode, int Shift);
```

You're already familiar with **Symbol**, **Timeframe**, **Mode** and **Shift** from earlier in the chapter. Let's start with **IndicatorName**. This is the name of the indicator file, exactly as it appears in the *Custom Indicators* list in the *Navigator* window. For example, "Slope Direction Line", or "super_signal".

`Indicator Parameters` is where we insert the parameters for the custom indicator. The *Inputs* tab in the *Custom Indicator Properties* window will show the parameters for the custom indicator. The icons to the left of each parameter will indicate the data type. If you don't have the `.mq4` file for an indicator, you'll have to determine the indicator parameters from this dialog.

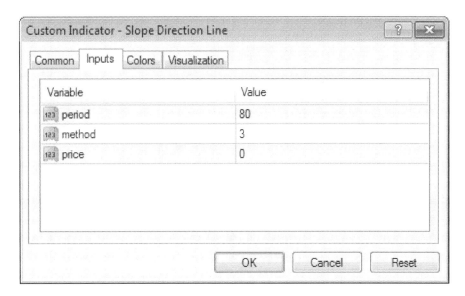

Fig 6.1 – The custom indicator input dialog

A easier way of finding the parameters is to check the **extern** variables at the beginning of the indicator source code file. All indicator parameters, their data types, and default values will be listed here, You can simply copy and paste this code to the external variables section of your expert advisor.

Each and every external variable in a custom indicator must have a counterpart parameter in the **iCustom()** function, and they must be in the order that they appear in the indicator. You can use a constant for parameters that do not need to be changed (such as informational strings, or non-essential settings).

Here's an example: The popular custom indicator *Slope Direction Line* has these external variables listed in the source code. We'll create external variables for these settings in our expert advisor:

```
//---- input parameters
extern int      period=80;
extern int      method=3;              // MODE_SMA
extern int      price=0;               // PRICE_CLOSE
```

We'll use the identifiers **SlopePeriod**, **SlopeMethod** and **SlopePrice** for the external variables in our expert advisor.

```
// External variables
extern int SlopePeriod = 80;
extern int SlopeMethod = 3;
extern int SlopePrice = 0;
```

Here is how the **iCustom()** function will look for this particular indicator, along with the external variables:

```
iCustom(NULL,0,"Slope Direction Line",SlopePeriod,SlopeMethod,SlopePrice,0,0);
```

NULL indicates that we are using the current chart symbol, and **0** is the current chart period. **"Slope Direction Line"** is the name of the indicator file. **SlopePeriod**, **SlopeMethod** and **SlopePrice** are the three indicator parameters. We are using the default **Mode** index of **0**, and the **Shift** is the current bar.

Although the Slope Direction Line indicator is drawn as a single line, it is actually composed of two different buffers. Depending on whether the indicator price is moving up or down, the color (and the buffer) change.

If you attach the indicator to a chart and view the *Data Window* in MetaTrader, you'll see two values for the Slope Direction Line. The first value displays a price when the indicator value is increasing. The line is blue by default. The second value displays a price when the indicator value is decreasing. This line is red by default.

We need to determine the **Mode** index for both of these lines. The easiest way to do this is to look at the source code. In the **init()** function, you will see several lines of code that are used to declare and set the properties for the indicator buffers:

Data Window	✕
⬜ GBPUSD,M5	
Date	2010.02.04
Time	23:50
Open	1.57619
High	1.57668
Low	1.57619
Close	1.57664
Volume	63
ƒ Slope Direction ...	1.5754
ƒ Value 2	

Fig 6.2 – Data Window

```
SetIndexBuffer(0, Uptrend);
SetIndexBuffer(1, Dntrend);
SetIndexBuffer(2, ExtMapBuffer);
...
SetIndexStyle(0,DRAW_LINE,STYLE_SOLID,2);
SetIndexStyle(1,DRAW_LINE,STYLE_SOLID,2);
```

The first **SetIndexBuffer()** function sets an indicator buffer with an index of 0, and uses the array **Uptrend**. We can guess from the array name that this applies to to the blue indicator line. The second function does likewise for for the array **DnTrend**. Note the **SetIndexStyle()** functions at the bottom that sets buffers 0 and 1 to draw a solid line.

The third buffer, with the index of 2 and the array **ExtMapBuffer**, is used for calculation only. We can therefore conclude that 0 and 1 are the buffer indexes that contain our indicator price information. Based on the array identifiers, 0 is the uptrend line, and 1 is the downtrend. Here is how we declare our indicators:

```
double SlopeUp = iCustom(NULL,0,"Slope Direction Line",SlopePeriod,SlopeMethod,
    SlopePrice,0,1);

double SlopeDown = iCustom(NULL,0,"Slope Direction Line",SlopePeriod,SlopeMethod,
    SlopePrice,1,1);
```

Note that the **Mode** parameter – the next to last one – has been set to the appropriate indicator buffer index – **0** for **SlopeUp**, and **1** for **SlopeDown**. The **Shift** parameter – the very last one – has been set to **1**, which checks the closing value of the last bar.

It's a good idea to double check that you're using the correct **Mode** parameters. Add a **Print()** function to your expert advisor, and run a back test in the Strategy Tester using "Open prices only" as the testing model. Make sure the **Shift** parameter is set to 1 in the **iCustom()** function.

```
Print("Slope Up: "+SlopeUp+", Slope Down: "+SlopeDown+" Time: "+TimeToStr(Time[1]));
```

The **Print()** function prints the value of our indicator buffers to the log, along with the time and date of the previous bar. You can view the log under the *Journal* tab in the Strategy Tester window. Here is the output of the **Print()** function in the log:

```
Slope Up: 2147483647.00000000, Slope Down: 1.50483900 Time: 2009.11.26 16:00
```

The value for **SlopeUp**, 2147483647, is a very large integer that represents the **EMPTY_VALUE** state of a custom indicator. You can actually use this as a trading condition. **SlopeDown** returns the indicator value of the previous bar. **Time** indicates the bar that we want to find on the chart.

Click the *Open Chart* button in the Strategy Tester window to open a chart with your indicator already applied. Find the bar indicated in the log by **Time**, and make sure the indicator values in the Data Window match those printed in the log. If not, adjust the **Mode** parameter in the **iCustom()** function until you find the correct buffer.

Here's how we would use the Slope Direction Line indicator in our expert advisor. If the slope is trending upward, **SlopeUp** will return a price value, while **SlopeDown** will return **EMPTY_VALUE**, or 2147483647. The opposite applies when the slope is trending downward.

```
if(SlopeUp != EMPTY_VALUE && SlopeDown == EMPTY_VALUE) // Buy
if(SlopeUp == EMPTY_VALUE && SlopeDown != EMPTY_VALUE) // Sell
```

These conditions simply check to see which line is equal to **EMPTY_VALUE**, and which line is not.

Indicator Constants

Time Frames

Many functions in MQL, including indicator and price functions, accept a time frame parameter. As indicated before, if we use a **Timeframe** parameter of 0, the current chart time frame will be used. If we wish to use a different time frame, we will need to specify the time frame in minutes. For example, M5 is 5, H1 is 60 and H4 is 240. We can also use constants to indicate the time frame:

- **PERIOD_M1** – 1 minute.

- **PERIOD_M5** – 5 minute.

- **PERIOD_M15** – 15 minute.

- **PERIOD_M30** – 30 minute.

- **PERIOD_H1** – 1 hour (60 minutes).

- **PERIOD_H4** – 4 hour (240 minutes).

- **PERIOD_D1** – Daily (1440 minutes).

Applied Price

The applied price indicator parameter indicates the price series to use when calculating the indicator value. You will generally use the close to calculate indicator values, although you may wish to use other values as well. Here is the list of price series and their associated constants, along with the integer value:

- **PRICE_CLOSE** – 0: Close price.

- **PRICE_OPEN** – 1: Open price.

- **PRICE_HIGH** – 2: High price.

- **PRICE_LOW** – 3: Low price.

- **PRICE_MEDIAN** – 4: Median price, *(High+Low)/2.*

- **PRICE_TYPICAL** – 5: Typical price, *(High+Low+Close)/3.*

- **PRICE_WEIGHTED** – 6: Weighted price, *(High+Low+Close+Close)/4.*

Moving Average Methods

Indicators that use a moving average as part of their calculation may have a parameter to adjust the moving average calculation method. The moving average line will be drawn differently depending on the calculation method. Here are the moving average method constants with their corresponding integer values:

- **MODE_SMA** – 0: Simple moving average. Calculates the mean of the price data.

- **MODE_EMA** – 1: Exponential moving average. Gives more weight to recent price data, and exponentially less weight to older price data. A very popular moving average.

- **MODE_SMMA** – 2: Smoothed moving average. A simple moving average calculated with a smoothing equation. Creates a smooth, but less responsive line.

- **MODE_LWMA** – 3: Linear weighted moving average. Similar to the exponential moving average, but gives increased weight to the most current price.

Evaluating Trade Conditions

We use the conditional operators `if` and `else` to evaluate our trading conditions. You've already seen these used in this book, but for you new programmers, a quick review is in order.

The `if` operator evaluates a true or false condition. If the condition is true, the code immediately after the `if` statement is executed. If the condition is false, it will skip ahead to the code following the if block:

```
if(BuyCondition == true)
  {
    OpenBuyOrder(...);
  }
```

If there is only one statement following the `if` operator, it can be written like this:

```
if(BuyCondition == true) OpenBuyOrder(...);
```

Multiple statements must be enclosed in braces.

The **else** operator evaluates an alternate condition, provided that the previous **if** statement(s) are false. You can combine **else** and **if** to create an alternate condition that will only be executed if it's true.

For example, this code evaluates three conditions in order. If one of them is true, only that block of code will be executed. If none of them are true, none of them will be executed:

```
if(Condition1 == true)        // Execute condition 1
else if(Condition2 == true)   // Execute condition 2
else if(Condition3 == true)   // Execute condition 3
```

The **else** operator can be used by itself at the end of an **if-else** sequence to indicate a condition that will be executed by default if all of the other if operators are false. As above, only one of the conditions will be executed:

```
if(Condition1 == true)        // Execute condition 1
else if(Condition2 == true)   // Execute condition 2
else
  {
     // Execute condition 3 if 1 and 2 are false
  }
```

If you have multiple **if** operators without any **else** operators, each one will be executed if it is true – it doesn't matter whether the subsequent **if** statement is true or false:

```
if(Condition1 == true)   // Execute condition 1
if(Condition2 == true)   // Execute condition 2
```

Relation Operations

We begin evaluating true and false conditions by comparing values using greater than, less than, equal to, not equal to and so on. Here's a list of relation operations:

- **== Equal To** – If x == y, the condition is true.

- **> Greater Than** – If x > y, the condition is true.

- **< Less Than** – If x < y, the condition is true.

- **>= Greater Than or Equal To** – If x >= y, the condition is true.

- **<= Less Than or Equal To** – if **x <= y**, the condition is true.

- **!= Not Equal To** – If **x != y**, the condition is true.

Note that the equal to operator (==) is not the same as the assignment operator (=)! The assignment operator is used when assigning a value to a variable. The equal to operator is used to evaluate a true/false condition. This is a common syntax error, and one you should watch out for.

You can compare any two values as long as they are of the same data type. You can compare a boolean value to the constants **true** or **false**. You can compare a string, integer or double variable to an appropriate constant value, or to another variable of the same type.

Boolean Operations

We use the boolean operators AND (**&&**) and OR (**||**) to combine relation operations. The AND operator evaluates whether all conditions are true. If so, the entire statement is true. If any of the conditions are false, the entire statement is false.

```
if(BooleanVar1 == true && Indicator1 > Indicator2)
   {
      // Open order
   }
```

If **BooleanVar1** is equal to true, and **Indicator1** is greater than **Indicator2**, the statement evaluates to **true**, and the code between the braces is run. If either of these conditions are false, the entire statement evaluates to **false**, and the code in the braces is not run. There can be any number of conditions combined together with the **&&** operator, and they must all evaluate to true.

The OR operator evaluates whether any one of the conditions are true. If at least one condition is true, the entire statement evaluates to **true**. If all of the conditions are false, the statement evaluates to **false**.

```
if(BooleanVar1 == true || Indicator1 > Indicator2)
```

If either **BooleanVar1** is equal to true, or **Indicator1** is greater than **Indicator2**, the statement is evaluated to **true**. If both of these conditions are false, the statement evaluates to **false**.

You can combine AND and OR operations to create more complex trading conditions. When doing so, use parentheses to establish the order of operations.

```
if((BooleanVar1 == true && Indicator1 > Indicator2) || BooleanVar1 == false)
```

The statement **(BooleanVar1 == true && Indicator1 > Indicator2)** is evaluated first. If both of these conditions are true, the statement evaluates to true, and we are left with an OR operation:

```
if(true || BooleanVar1 == false)
```

This statement automatically evaluates to true, since one of the conditions is already true. But what if **(BooleanVar1 == true && Indicator1 > Indicator2)** evaluates to false?

```
if(false || BooleanVar1 == false)
```

If the condition **BooleanVar1 == false** evaluates to true, then the entire statement is true. (In other words, if **BooleanVar1** is set to **false**, that condition evaluates to true.) Otherwise, the statement is false.

It's possible to create complex boolean operations using AND, OR and parentheses to control the order of operations. Be sure to watch the locations of your parentheses, as one wrong parenthesis can cause the statement to evaluate differently, and a missing parenthesis could lead to some tedious debugging.

Turning An Indicator On and Off

You can use the AND/OR example in the previous section to turn an indicator on and off. Let's say your EA uses multiple indicators, and you'd like to be able to switch indicators on and off. Here's how we do it. First, let's declare an external boolean variable to use as the on/off switch. We'll use the stochastic indicator in this example:

```
extern bool UseStochastic = true;
```

We define two sets of conditions for our indicator – an "on" state and an "off" state. The on state consists of the on/off variable being set to true, along with the order opening condition. The off state simply consists of the on/off variable being set to false.

```
if((UseStochastic == true && Kline > Dline) || UseStochastic == false)
  {
    // Buy order
  }
```

The statement **(UseStochastic == true && Kline > Dline)** is our "on" state. If the **UseStochastic** external variable is set to **true**, and the trading condition **Kline > Dline** evaluates to **true**, then the stochastic order condition will be true.

UseStochastic == false is our "off" state. If the **UseStochastic** external variable is set to false, then **(UseStochastic == true && Kline > Dline)** evaluates to false, while **UseStochastic == false** evaluates to true.

Since the on and off states are linked by an OR operator, only one of them has to be true to make the whole statement true. So as long as either a.) the indicator is on, and the order placement condition is valid; or b.) the indicator is off; the entire statement will be true, and any remaining order conditions can be evaluated.

Let's add a second trade condition to our stochastic condition – the moving average cross:

```
if(((UseStochastic == true && Kline > Dline) || UseStochastic == false)
    && FastMA > SlowMA)
```

In this example, we've added the moving average cross condition, **FastMA > SlowMA**. Note that we added another set of parentheses around the stochastic condition, since the entire statement in the parentheses needs to be evaluated first.

First, we evaluate the statement inside the innermost set of parentheses: **(UseStochastic == true && Kline > Dline)**. If the **UseStochastic** parameter is set to **true**, and **Kline > Dline** evaluates to **true**, the first part of the statement is **true**.

```
if((true || UseStochastic == false) && FastMA > SlowMA)
```

The condition **UseStochastic == false** evaluates to **false**. We are left with an OR operation, and since one of the conditions is already true, the entire stochastic condition evaluates to **true**:

```
if((true || false) && FastMA > SlowMA)

if(true && FastMA > SlowMA)
```

If **FastMA > SlowMA** evaluates to **true**, the entire trading condition is true, and the order is placed. If it is false, the statement evaluates to **false**, and the order is not placed.

Now, what happens if the stochastic trading condition is false? If **UseStochastic** is set to true, and **Kline > Dline** evaluates to false, the entire condition becomes false:

107

```
if((false || UseStochastic == false) && FastMA > SlowMA)

if((false || false) && FastMA > SlowMA)

if(false && FastMA > SlowMA)
```

Regardless of how **FastMA > SlowMA** evaluates, the entire trade condition is false.

Now lets say that **UseStochastic** is set to false. In this case, the statement **(UseStochastic == true && Kline > Dline)** evaluates to false:

```
if((false || UseStochastic == false) && FastMA > SlowMA)
```

Since the statement **UseStochastic == false** is true, the stochastic condition evaluates to true.

```
if((false || true) && FastMA > SlowMA)

if(true && FastMA > SlowMA)
```

Which means that if **FastMA > SlowMA** also evaluates to true, the order will be placed. In this case, the stochastic condition wasn't even considered, aside from evaluating the on/off state of the indicator.

Comparing Indicator Values Across Bars

Sometimes you will need to compare the indicator value of the current or most recently closed bar to the indicator value of a previous bar. For example, let's say you want to know whether a moving average is going up or down. To do this, we compare the indicator reading of the current bar to that of the previous bar.

We use the **Shift** parameter of an indicator function to determine which bar to return the indicator value for. The **Shift** parameter is always the last parameter in an indicator function. The current bar has a shift of 0, the previous bar has a shift of 1, and so on. The moving average functions below will return a moving average value for the current and the previous bar:

```
double MA = iMA(NULL,0,MAPeriod,0,MAMethod,MAPrice,0);
double LastMA = iMA(NULL,0,MAPeriod,0,MAMethod,MAPrice,1);
```

In this example, `MA` is the variable that holds the current bar's indicator value, while `LastMA` holds the previous bar's indicator value. Note that the `Shift` parameter is 0 for the current bar, and 1 for the previous bar.

Here is the code to determine whether a moving average line is moving up or down:

```
if(MA > LastMA)
   {
      // MA is going up
   }

else if(MA < LastMA)
   {
      // MA is going down
   }
```

If the indicator value of the current bar (`MA`) is greater than the value of the previous bar (`LastMA`), we can conclude that the indicator is moving up. The reverse is true when the current bar's indicator value is less than the previous bar's indicator value.

By comparing the indicator value of a previous bar to the current one, we can determine whether the indicator has recently crossed above or below a certain value, such the overbought/oversold levels of an oscillator, or another indicator line.

For example, let's say your trading system gives a trade signal when the stochastic passes above 30 or below 70. Here is the code to check for that:

```
double Stoch = iStochastic(NULL,0,KPeriod,DPeriod,Slowing,MAMethod,Price,0,0);
double LastStoch = iStochastic(NULL,0,KPeriod,DPeriod,Slowing,MAMethod,Price,0,1);

if(Stoch > 30 && LastStoch < 30)
   {
      // Open buy order
   }

if(Stoch < 70 && LastStoch > 70)
   {
      // Open sell order
   }
```

`Stoch` is the indicator value of the current bar, while `LastStoch` is the indicator value of the previous bar. If `Stoch` is greater than 30 and `LastStoch` is less than 30, we can conclude that the indicator crossed above the oversold level within the last bar. By reversing the comparison operators, we can check for a recent cross below a constant value, such as the overbought level of 70.

Here's another example using moving averages. We'll create a condition to open an order only when the **FastMA** and the **SlowMA** have crossed within the last bar:

```
double FastMA = iMA(NULL,0,FastMAPeriod,0,0,0,0);
double SlowMA = iMA(NULL,0,SlowMAPeriod,0,0,0,0);

double LastFastMA = iMA(NULL,0,FastMAPeriod,0,0,0,1);
double LastSlowMA = iMA(NULL,0,SlowMAPeriod,0,0,0,1);


if(FastMA > SlowMA && LastFastMA <= LastSlowMA
   && BuyMarketCount(Symbol(),MagicNumber) == 0)
   {
     // Open buy order
   }

if(FastMA < SlowMA && LastFastMA >= LastSlowMA
   && SellMarketCount(Symbol(),MagicNumber) == 0)
   {
     // Open sell order
   }
```

In this example, we're comparing the relationship of two indicators to each other. **LastFastMA** and **LastSlowMA** return the moving average values for the previous bar. If **LastFastMA** is less than (or equal to) **LastSlowMA**, and **FastMA** is currently greater than **SlowMA**, then we know that the fast moving average line has crossed above the slow moving average line within the last bar.

This provides a reliable trading signal, since we can limit our order placement to right after the cross occurs. You can change the **Shift** value for the **LastFastMA** and **LastSlowMA** functions if you want to increase the number of bars to look back when finding an indicator cross.

We've added the **LastFastMA** and **LastSlowMA** comparison to our buy and sell order conditions in our expert advisor. We can now remove the **BuyTicket** and **SellTicket** check, since this method is more reliable that checking a stored order ticket number. We also don't have to worry about orders being placed well after the cross has occurred. See the expert advisor code in Appendix C to view all of the changes.

Chapter 7
Working with Time and Date

Datetime Variables

Internally, the **datetime** variable is represented as the number of seconds elapsed since January 1, 1970. For example, June 15, 2009 at 0:00 (midnight) would be 1245024000. The advantage of datetime format is that it makes past and future time comparisons and mathematical manipulations very easy.

For example, if you wanted to check whether one date comes before or after another date, you would do a simple relational operation. Let's say that **StartDate** is June 15, 2009 at 14:00, and **EndDate** is June 16, 2009 at 5:00.

```
if(StartDate < EndDate) // Result is true
if(StartDate > EndDate) // Result is false
```

Another advantage is that you can add or subtract time from a particular date, simply by adding or subtracting the appropriate number of seconds. If you want to add 24 hours to **StartDate**, simply add the number of seconds in a day:

```
datetime AddDay = StartDate + 86400;
```

If you're planning to do a lot of mathematical manipulation with datetime variables, it might be a good idea to declare some integer constants to represent certain units of time:

```
#define SEC_H1 3600    // Seconds in an hour
#define SEC_D1 86400   // Seconds in a day
```

The disadvantage of **datetime** format is that it is not very readable. You can't look at a value such as 1245024000 and automatically tell that it represents June 15, 2009 at 0:00. For this, we use conversion functions to convert datetime to and from a more readable form.

Datetime Constants

A datetime constant is a date and time presented in the following string format: **yyyy.mm.dd hh:mm**. For example, June 15, 2009 at 0:00 would be **2009.06.15 00:00**. There are other acceptable formats for datetime constants: the MQL Reference topic *Basics – Data Types – Datetime constants* has more information. We'll use the format presented above, since it is the only one that can be easily converted.

To convert a datetime variable to a string constant, use the function **TimeToStr()**. Here is the syntax:

```
string TimeToStr(datetime Time, int Output = TIME_DATE|TIME_MINUTES);
```

- **Time** – A datetime variable expressed as the number of seconds elapsed since January 1, 1970.

- **Output** – An optional parameter that outputs the constant as date only, hour and minute only; hour, minute and seconds; or any combination of date and time. Valid input values are :

  - **TIME_DATE** – Outputs the date, for example, **2009.06.15**

  - **TIME_MINUTES** – Outputs hour and minute, for example, **05:30**

  - **TIME_SECONDS** – Outputs hour, minute and seconds, for example, **05:30:45**

To output the string constant in the default **yyyy.mm.dd hh:mm** format, leave **Output** blank. If you only want the date, or the hour and minute (or seconds), use the appropriate argument. In this example, we'll assume that **StartTime** is equal to **2009.06.15 05:30:45**.

```
TimeToStr(StartTime,TIME_DATE)              // Returns "2009.06.15"
TimeToStr(StartTime,TIME_SECONDS)           // Returns "05:30:45"
TimeToStr(StartTime,TIME_MINUTES)           // Returns "05:30"
TimeToStr(StartTime,TIME_DATE|TIME_SECONDS) // Returns "2009.06.15 05:30:45"
TimeToStr(StartTime)                         // Returns "2009.06.15 05:30"
```

We can construct a datetime constant using string concatenation, and convert it to a datetime variable using the function **StrToTime()**. The syntax is identical to **TimeToStr()** above, but without the **Output** parameter. The string constant must be in the format **yyyy.mm.dd hh:mm** to be converted correctly.

Here's an example of how we can assemble a datetime constant using integers, convert those integers to string format, and convert the string to a datetime variable. First, we'll declare some external variables to set a time and date:

```
extern int UseMonth = 6;
extern int UseDay = 15;
extern int UseHour = 5;
extern int UseMinute = 30;
```

113

Next, we create the string constant using the **StringConcatenate()** function, and finally convert the string to **datetime** format using **StrToTime()**.

```
string DateConstant = StringConcatenate(Year(),".",UseMonth,".",UseDay," ",
    UseHour,":",UseMinute);                              // DateConstant is "2009.6.15 05:30"

datetime StartTime = StrToTime(DateConstant);       // StartTime is "1245043800"
```

Note that in the **StringConcatenate()** function, we use **Year()** to return the current year instead of using an external variable. You can use functions like **Month()**, **Day()** and so on to insert current time values. We'll cover these in the next section.

Date and Time Functions

There are two functions that return the current time: **TimeCurrent()** returns the current server time, while **TimeLocal()** returns your local computer time. You can use whichever you prefer. You may want to create a boolean external variable to choose between the two:

```
extern bool UseLocalTime = true;
```

Here is the code to assign either the current local time or the current server time to a variable named **CurrentTime**.

```
if(UseLocalTime == true) datetime CurrentTime = TimeLocal();     // Local time
else CurrentTime = TimeCurrent();                                // Server time
```

Sometimes you may just need to retrieve a part of the current time, such as the hour or day. Here is the list of the most useful functions you can use to return current time values. All of these functions use the server time – not your local computer time. The return value is of type integer:

- **Year()** – The current four-digit year, for example, 2009.

- **Month()** – The current month of the year from 1 to 12.

- **Day()** – The current day of the month from 1 to 31.

- **DayOfWeek()** – An integer representing the current day of the week. Sunday is 0, Monday is 1, Friday is 5 and so on.

- **Hour()** – The current hour in 24 hour time, from 0 to 23. For example, 3am is 3, and 3pm is 15.

- **Minute()** – The current minute from 0 to 59.

You can also retrieve these values from any datetime variable using a different set of functions. These functions require a datetime variable as the only parameter, but otherwise work just like the functions above. If you want to retrieve a time value from `TimeLocal()`, use the output of the `TimeLocal()` function as the argument for the functions below:

- `TimeYear()` – The four-digit year of the specified datetime value.

- `TimeMonth()` – The month of the specified datetime value from 1 to 12.

- `TimeDay()` – The day of the month of the specified datetime value from 1 to 31.

- `TimeDayOfWeek()` – An integer representing the day of the week of the specified datetime value. Sunday is 0, Monday is 1, Friday is 5 and so on.

- `TimeHour()` – The hour of the specified datetime value in 24 hour time, from 0 to 23.

- `TimeMinute()` – The minute of the specified datetime value from 0 to 59.

Here are a few examples of the usage of these functions. Let's assume that `TimeLocal()` is equal to `2009.06.15 05:30.`

```
datetime CurrentTime = TimeLocal();

int GetMonth = TimeMonth(CurrentTime);          // Returns 6
int GetHour = TimeHour(CurrentTime);            // Returns 5
int GetWeekday = TimeDayOfWeek(CurrentTime);    // Returns 1 for Monday
```

Creating A Simple Timer

One very handy thing we can do with time and date in MQL is to add a timer to our expert advisor. Some traders like to limit their trading to the most active hours of the day, such as the London & New York sessions. Others may wish to avoid trading during volatile market events, such as news reports and NFP.

To construct a timer, we need to specify a start time and an end time. We will use external integer variables to input the time parameters. We will create a datetime constant string, and convert that to a datetime variable. We will then compare our start and end times to the current time. If the current time is greater than the start time, but less than the end time, trading will be allowed.

Here are the external variables we're going to use. We'll set a variable to turn the timer on and off, as well as to select the current time (server or local). We have month, day, hour and minute settings for both the start and end times:

```
extern bool UseTimer = true;
extern bool UseLocalTime = false;

extern int StartMonth = 6;
extern int StartDay = 15;
extern int StartHour = 7;
extern int StartMinute = 0;

extern int EndMonth = 6;
extern int EndDay = 15;
extern int EndHour = 2;
extern int EndMinute = 30;
```

And here is the code for checking whether to allow trading or not. The variable **TradeAllowed** determines whether to open new trades. If **UseTimer** is set to false, **TradeAllowed** is automatically set to true. Otherwise, we evaluate our start and end times in relation to the current time to see if we will allow trading or not.

```
if(UseTimer == true)
   {
     // Convert start time
     string StartConstant = StringConcatenate(Year(),".",StartMonth,".",StartDay," ",
       StartHour,":",StartMinute);

     datetime StartTime = StrToTime(StartConstant);

     if(StartMonth == 12 && StartDay == 31 && EndMonth == 1) int EndYear = Year() + 1;
     else EndYear = Year();

     // Convert end time
     string EndConstant = StringConcatenate(EndYear,".",EndMonth,".",EndDay," ",
       EndHour,":",EndMinute);

     datetime EndTime = StrToTime(EndConstant);

     // Choose local or server time
     if(UseLocalTime == true) datetime CurrentTime = TimeLocal();
     else CurrentTime = TimeCurrent();

     // Check for trade condition
     if(StartTime <= CurrentTime && EndTime > CurrentTime)
       {
         bool TradeAllowed = true;
       }
     else TradeAllowed = false;
   }
else TradeAllowed = true;
```

We start by converting our start time to a datetime variable, **StartTime**. The statement **if(StartMonth == 12 && StartDay == 31 && EndMonth == 1)** checks to see if the start date is the last day of the year, and if the end day is after the first of the next year. If so, it automatically increments the end year by 1. Otherwise we use the current year for **EndYear**.

Next, we convert the end time to the datetime variable **EndTime** and choose which **CurrentTime** we want to use, server or local. The final **if** block checks to see if the current time is between the start and end times. If so, **TradeAllowed** is set to true.

Now we need to add the code to control trade execution. The easiest way to do this is to add an **if** block around our order opening routines:

```
// Begin trade block
if(TradeAllowed == true)
  {
    // Buy Order
    if(FastMA > SlowMA && BuyTicket == 0 && BuyOrderCount(Symbol(),MagicNumber) == 0)
      {
        // Buy order code omitted for brevity
      }

    // Sell Order
    if(FastMA < SlowMA && SellTicket == 0 && SellOrderCount(Symbol(),MagicNumber) == 0)
      {
        // Sell order code omitted for brevity
      }
  } // End trade block
```

There are many more ways to create timers – for example, you could use the day of the week instead of the month and day, or set trade times relative to the current day. We'll leave it to you, the reader, to create a timer that is appropriate for your needs.

Execute On Bar Open

By default, expert advisors run in real-time, on every tick. But in some cases, it may be better to check trading conditions only once per bar. By waiting for the current bar to close, we can be sure that the condition has occurred and that the signal is valid. In comparison, by executing trades in real-time, we may be more susceptible to false signals.

Trading once per bar also means that the results in the Strategy Tester will be more accurate and relevant. Due to the inherent limitations of MetaTrader's Strategy Tester, using "Every tick" as the testing model will produce unreliable back testing results, due to the fact that ticks are often modeled from M1 data. The trades that occur in live trading will not necessarily correspond to trade made in the Strategy Tester.

But by placing our trades on the close on the bar and using "Open prices only" as the testing model, we can get testing results that more accurately reflect real-time trades. The disadvantage of trading once per bar is that trades may be executed late, especially if there is a lot of price movement over the course of the bar. It's basically a trade-off between responsiveness and reliability.

To check the trade conditions once per bar, we must examine the time stamp of the current bar. We will save this time stamp to a global variable. Upon each execution of the expert advisor, we will compare the saved time stamp to the current time stamp. Once the time stamp of the current bar changes, indicating that a new bar has opened, we will then check the trading conditions.

We must also adjust the shift parameter of our indicator functions, price functions and arrays to return the value of the previous bar. If an indicator function or price array is set to check the current bar, we will shift the bar index by 1 to check the previous bar instead. All indicators and price arrays must have their shift parameters incremented by 1.

Technically, we are checking trading conditions on the first tick of a new bar, while examining the closing value of the previous bar. We do not check the currently opened bar when executing once per bar.

Here is the code to check for the opening of a new bar. First, we declare an external variable named **CheckOncePerBar** to turn this feature on and off. Then we declare a **datetime** global variable to store the time stamp of the current bar – this will be **CurrentTimeStamp**.

In the **init()** function, we will assign the time stamp of the current bar to **CurrentTimeStamp**. This will delay the trade condition check until the opening of the next bar:

```
// External variables
extern bool CheckOncePerBar = true;


// Global variables
datetime CurrentTimeStamp;


// Init function
int init()
  {
    CurrentTimeStamp = Time[0];
  }
```

Here is the code that goes at the beginning of our **start()** function, just after the timer. The integer variable **BarShift** will determine whether to set the **Shift** value of our indicator and price functions to the current bar or the previous bar. The boolean variable **NewBar** will determine whether we will check our trade conditions:

```
if(CheckOncePerBar == true)
  {
     int BarShift = 1;
     if(CurrentTimeStamp != Time[0])
       {
          CurrentTimeStamp = Time[0];
          bool NewBar = true;
       }
     else NewBar = false;
  }
else
  {
     NewBar = true;
     BarShift = 0;
  }
```

If **CheckOncePerBar** is set to **true**, we will first set **BarShift** to 1. This will set the **Shift** parameter of all indicator and price functions/arrays to the previous bar.

Next, we compare the value of **CurrentTimeStamp** variable to **Time[0]**, which is the time stamp of the current bar. If the two values do not match, we will assign the value of **Time[0]** to **CurrentTimeStamp** and set **NewBar** to true. The trading conditions will be checked shortly thereafter.

On subsequent runs, **CurrentTimeStamp** and **Time[0]** will match, which means that **NewBar** will be set to false. The trade conditions will not be checked until a new bar opens. Once a new bar opens, **Time[0]** will be a different value than **CurrentTimeStamp**, and **NewBar** will be set to true once again.

If **CheckOncePerBar** is set to **false**, **NewBar** will automatically be set to **true**, and **BarShift** will be set to **0**. This will check the trading conditions on every tick, as before.

The **BarShift** variable will need to be assigned to the **Shift** parameter of any indicator functions, price functions or arrays that reference the most recent bar. Here are some examples of how this would be applied:

```
double FastMA = iMA(NULL,0,FastMAPeriod,0,0,0,BarShift);

if(Close[BarShift] > Open[BarShift])

double UseLow = iLow(NULL,0,BarShift);
```

You should recognize these examples from before. Instead of checking the current bar, we will check the bar that just closed, *i.e.* the previous bar. If you need to reference a bar previous to the last closed bar, simply add the current shift parameter to **BarShift**:

```
double LastFastMA = iMA(NULL,0,FastMAPeriod,0,0,0,BarShift+1);
```

If you don't anticipate ever needing to run your expert advisor once per bar, you won't need to add this code. But for many indicator-based trading systems, this can make your trading and back testing results more reliable.

To control the execution of trades, we need to check the value of **NewBar** before the order placement routines. We can do this using the **if** block we placed earlier for the timer:

```
// Begin trade block
if(TradeAllowed == true && NewBar == true)
  {
    // Buy Order
    if(FastMA > SlowMA && BuyTicket == 0 && BuyOrderCount(Symbol(),MagicNumber) == 0)
      {
        // Buy order code omitted for brevity
      }

    // Sell Order
    if(FastMA < SlowMA && SellTicket == 0 && SellOrderCount(Symbol(),MagicNumber) == 0)
      {
        // Sell order code omitted for brevity
      }

  } // End trade block
```

Chapter 8
Tips and Tricks

In this chapter, we will cover additional features that may be useful in your expert advisors.

Escape Characters

If you want to add quotes or a backslash character to a string constant, you'll need to *escape* the character using a backslash (\). For example, if you need to insert a double quote, the escape character will be \". For a single quote, the escape character is \'. For a backslash, use two backslashes as the escape character: \\

```
string EscQuotes = "This string has \"escaped double quotes\"";
// Output: This string has "escaped double quotes"

string EscQuote = "This string has \'escaped single quotes\'";
// Output: This string has 'escaped single quotes'

string EscSlash = "This string has an escaped backslash \\";
// Output: This string has an escaped backslash \
```

If you need a string to span multiple lines, use the escape character \n to add a newline:

```
string NewLine = "This string has \n a newline";
// Output:   This string has
            a newline
```

Using Chart Comments

You can print text in the top left hand corner of the chart using the `Comment()` function. This can be used to print status information, indicator settings or any other information you may find useful.

One method for displaying chart comments is to declare several string variables and concatenate them together with newline characters. One string can be used to display settings, another to display information messages or order status, etc. The concatenated string will be passed to the `Comment()` function. Place the `Comment()` function at the end of the `start()` function to update the chart comment:

```
string SettingsComment = "FastMAPeriod: "+FastMAPeriod+" SlowMAPeriod: "+SlowMAPeriod;
string StatusComment = "Buy order placed";

Comment(SettingsComment+"\n"+StatusComment);
```

We declare and set the values of the **SettingsComment** and **StatusComment** strings inside the **start()** function. At the end of the start function, we call the **Comment()** function and use it to print our comments to the chart. We use a newline character (**\n**) to separate the comments into two lines.

```
GBPUSD,M5  1.56379 1.56394 1.56371 1.56389
FastMAPeriod: 10 SlowMAPeriod: 20
Buy order placed
```

Fig 8.1: Chart comment using a newline character

Check Settings

There are several expert advisor properties that must be enabled before the expert advisor may be allowed to trade. These settings are located under the *Common* tab in the *Expert Properties* dialog.

The setting *Allow live trading* must be enabled before trading can commence. If it is not enabled, a frowning face will appear in the top right hand corner of the chart, next to the expert advisor name. You can check for this condition in your EA by using the **IsTradeAllowed()** function. If it returns false, the setting *Allow live trading* is disabled.

If you'd like to display a message to the user indicating that this setting should be activated, you can do as follows:

```
if(IsTradeAllowed() == false) Alert("Enable the setting \'Allow live trading\' in the
    Expert Properties!");
```

If your expert advisor uses an external **.ex4** library, the setting *Allow import of external experts* must be enabled in the Expert Properties. You can check for this using the **IsLibrariesAllowed()** function:

```
if(IsLibrariesAllowed() == false) Alert("Enable the setting \'Allow import of external
    experts\' in the Expert Properties!");
```

The same thing can be done for DLLs using the **IsDllsAllowed()** function:

```
if(IsDllsAllowed() == false) Alert("Enable the setting \'Allow DLL imports\' in the
    Expert Properties!");
```

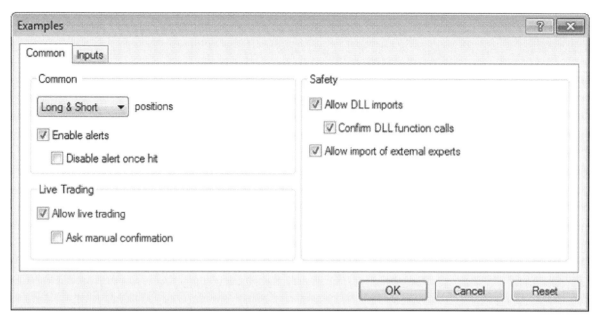

Fig. 8.2 – Common tab of Expert Advisor Properties dialog.

You can view all of the terminal checkup functions in the MQL Reference under *Checkup*.

Demo or Account Limitations

You may decide at some point to sell your profitable expert advisor to other traders. You may also want to provide a demo version for potential buyers to test. To prevent your EA from being freely distributed or traded by unauthorized persons, you'll want to incorporate some kind of account limitations that limit the usage of the EA to authorized buyers. You may even want to limit usage to a particular broker.

To limit usage to a demo account, use the **IsDemo()** function to check whether the currently active account is a demo account. If the current account is not a demo account, we will display an alert and halt the execution of the EA.

```
if(IsDemo() == false)
  {
    Alert("This EA only for use on a demo account!");
    return(0);
  }
```

You can use the account functions **AccountName()**, **AccountNumber()** and **AccountBroker()** to check the account name, number and broker respectively. Limiting usage by account number is a common and easy to implement method of protection:

```
int CustomerAccount = 123456;

if(AccountNumber() != CustomerAccount)
  {
    Alert("Account number does not match!");
    return(0);
  }
```

You can use **AccountName()** or **AccountBroker()** in a similar manner. For **AccountBroker()**, you'll first need to use a **Print()** statement to retrieve the correct return value from the broker. This value will be printed in the experts log.

If you do decide to sell an EA commercially, be aware that MQL files are notoriously easy to decompile. There are various methods you can use to make it more difficult for hackers to crack your EA, such as placing functions in external libraries or DLLs. But ultimately, there is little protection against a determined cracker.

MessageBox()

So far in this book, we've been using the built-in **Alert()** function to display error messages. But what if you want to customize your alert dialogs, or request input from the user? The **MessageBox()** function will allow you to create a custom pop-up dialog using Windows API functions.

To use the **MessageBox()** function, we must first **#include** the **WinUser32.mqh** file that is installed with MetaTrader. This file imports functions from the Windows **user32.dll** file and defines constants necessary for the **MessageBox()** function to work. Here is the syntax for the **MessageBox()** function:

```
int MessageBox(string Text, string Title, int Flags);
```

To use the **MessageBox()** function, we must define the **Text** to appear in the pop-up dialog, along with a **Title** that appears in the title bar. We will also need to specify **Flags** that indicate which buttons and icons should appear in our pop-up. If no flags are specified, an OK button will be the default. Flags must be separated by the pipe (|) character.

Here's an example of a message box with Yes/No buttons and a question mark icon:

```
// Preprocessor directives
#include <WinUser32.mqh>


// start() function
int YesNoBox = MessageBox("Place a Trade?","Trade Confirmation",
  MB_YESNO|MB_ICONQUESTION);

if(YesNoBox == IDYES)
  {
    // Place Order
  }
```

The flag **MB_YESNO** specifies that we will be using Yes/No buttons in our message box, while the **MB_ICONQUESTION** flag places the question mark icon in the dialog box. The integer variable **YesNoBox** holds the return value of the **MessageBox()** functions, which will indicate which button was pressed.

If the Yes button was pressed, the value of **YesNoBox** will be **IDYES**, and an order will be placed. If the No button was pressed, the return flag will be **IDNO**. You can use the return value of **MessageBox()** as input to determine a course of action, such as placing an order.

Fig. 8.3 – Popup dialog created using the MessageBox() function

What follows is a partial list of flags to use in your message boxes. For a complete list, please see the MQL Reference topic *Standard Constants – MessageBox*.

Button Flags

These flags specify which buttons appear in your message box.

- **MB_OKCANCEL** – OK and Cancel buttons.

- **MB_YESNO** – Yes and No buttons.

- **MB_YESNOCANCEL** – Yes, No and Cancel buttons.

Icon Flags

These flags specify icons that appear next to the text in the message box.

- **MB_ICONSTOP** – A stop sign icon.

- **MB_ICONQUESTION** – A question mark icon.

- **MB_ICONEXCLAMATION** – An exclamation point icon.

- **MB_ICONINFORMATION** – An information icon.

Return Flags

These flags are the return value of the `MessageBox()` function, and indicate which button was pressed.

- **IDOK** – The OK button was pressed.

- **IDCANCEL** – The Cancel button was pressed.

- **IDYES** – The Yes button was pressed

- **IDNO** – The No button was pressed.

Email Alerts

Your expert advisor can alert you by email about placed trades, potential trade setups and more. The function `SendMail()` will send an email with the subject and body of your choice to the email address that is listed in the *Tools – Options* dialog under the *Email* tab.

In the Email tab, you must first specify the SMTP mail server with port number – for example: *mail.yourdomain.com:25* -- along with a username and password, if required. Check with your ISP or hosting provider for this information.

You can use any email address in the *From* field. The *To* field is the email address to send messages to. Be sure to check the *Enable* setting at the top to enable the sending of messages.

The `SendMail()` function has two arguments: the first is the subject line of the email, and the second is the contents of the email itself. You can use newlines, escaped characters, variables and constants within the body of your email.

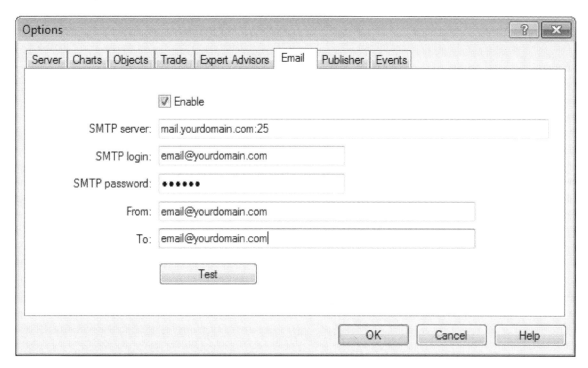

Fig. 8.4 – The Email settings under *Tools – Options*.

Here's an example of **SendMail()** usage:

```
string EmailSubject = "Buy order placed";
string EmailBody = "Buy order "+Ticket+" placed on "+Symbol()+" at "+Ask;
// Sample output: "Buy order 12584 placed on EURUSD at 1.4544"

SendMail(EmailSubject,EmailBody);
```

Retry on Error

Throughout this book, we've tried to verify order parameters before attempting to place an order, so as to avoid common error messages due to incorrect settings or prices. However, errors may still occur due to requotes, trade context busy or server issues. These errors can't always be avoided, but we can attempt to place the order again when this happens.

To retry an order on an error, we will place the **OrderSend()** function inside a **while** loop. If **OrderSend()** does not return a ticket number, we will retry the order again:

```
int Ticket = 0;
while(Ticket <= 0)
   {
      Ticket = OrderSend(Symbol(),OP_BUY,LotSize,OpenPrice,UseSlippage,
         BuyStopLoss,BuyTakeProfit);
   }
```

We declare the variable for the ticket number first, in this case **Ticket**. As long as **Ticket** is not greater than 0, the **while** loop with the **OrderSend()** function will execute over and over. There's one problem with this loop though. In case of a coding error or some other uncorrected trading error, the loop will iterate indefinitely, and your expert advisor will hang. We can alleviate this by adding a maximum number of retries:

```
int Retries = 0;
int MaxRetries = 5;

int Ticket = 0;
while(Ticket <= 0)
   {
      Ticket = OrderSend(Symbol(),OP_BUY,LotSize,OpenPrice,UseSlippage,BuyStopLoss,
         BuyTakeProfit);
      if(Retries <= MaxRetries) Retries++;
      else break;
   }
```

We declare a variable to use as a retry counter (**Retries**), and a maximum retry setting (**MaxRetries**). As long as we have not exceeded **MaxRetries**, the **Retries** variable is incremented and the loop iterates again. As soon as **MaxRetries** is reached, the **break** operator ends the loop. After this, you can alert the user of the error condition as necessary.

If you want to make the retry loop dependent on a particular error condition, we can check the error code against a list and return a value of true if there is a match. This function contains some common error codes that indicate a condition where a trade could be successfully retried:

```
bool ErrorCheck(int ErrorCode)
   {
      switch(ErrorCode)
         {
            case 128:        // Trade timeout
            return(true);

            case 136:        // Off quotes
            return(true);
```

```
         case 138:        // Requotes
         return(true);

         case 146:        // Trade context busy
         return(true);

         default:
         return(false);
      }
   }
```

This function uses the **switch** operator. We are looking for a **case** label whose value matches the expression assigned to the switch operator (in this example, **ErrorCode**). If a matching **case** is found, the code after **case** is executed. If no **case** label matches, then the code after the **default** label is executed.

When a **case** match is found, the **switch** block must be exited with a **break** or **return** operator. In this example, we are using the **return** operator to return a true/false value back to the calling function. The **switch** operator can be useful for evaluating a match for an integer constant, but its utility is rather limited.

Here is how we use **ErrorCheck()** to conditionally retry an order placement:

```
   int Retries;
   int MaxRetries = 5;

   int Ticket;
   while(Ticket <= 0)
      {
         Ticket = OrderSend(Symbol(),OP_BUY,LotSize,OpenPrice,UseSlippage,BuyStopLoss,
            BuyTakeProfit);

         if(Ticket == -1) int ErrCode = GetLastError();
         if(Retries <= MaxRetries && ErrorCheck(ErrCode) == true) Retries++;
         else break;
      }
```

If the **Ticket** returns **-1**, indicating that an error has occurred, we retrieve the error code using **GetLastError()**. We pass the error code to our **ErrorCheck()** function above. If the error code matches any of the errors in the error check function, **ErrorCheck()** will return true, and the **OrderSend()** function will be retried up to 5 times.

Using Order Comments As an Identifier

We've been using the "magic number" as an order identifier that uniquely identifies orders as being placed by a particular expert advisor. If your expert advisor places multiple orders at one time, and you want to be able to handle each of those orders differently, you can use the order comment as an optional identifier.

For example, lets say your expert advisor will place two types of orders. You want to be able to modify or close these orders separately. You'll want to use two **OrderSend()** functions and place a different order comment with each one. Then, when selecting orders using the order loop in chapter 5, you'll use **OrderComment()** as one of the conditions for locating orders to modify or close.

```
string OrderComment1 = "First order";
string OrderComment2 = "Second order";

// Order placement
int Ticket1 = OrderSend(Symbol(),OP_BUY,LotSize,OpenPrice,UseSlippage,BuyStopLoss,
  BuyTakeProfit,OrderComment1,MagicNumber,0,Green);

int Ticket2 = OrderSend(Symbol(),OP_BUY,LotSize,OpenPrice,UseSlippage,BuyStopLoss,
  BuyTakeProfit,OrderComment2,MagicNumber,0,Green);

// Order modification
for(int Counter = 0; Counter <= OrdersTotal()-1; Counter++)
  {
    OrderSelect(Counter,SELECT_BY_POS);

    if(OrderMagicNumber() == MagicNumber && OrderSymbol() == Symbol()
      && OrderComment() == OrderComment1)
      {
        // Modify first order
      }

    else if(OrderMagicNumber() == MagicNumber && OrderSymbol() == Symbol()
      && OrderComment() == OrderComment2)
      {
        // Modify second order
      }
  }
```

We declare two string variables to use as order comments. The **OrderSend()** functions place two orders, each with a different order comment. The example order modification loop that follows uses the **OrderComment()** function as a condition when selecting orders to modify.

You can use the **OrderComment()** check to close orders independently of other orders, use different trailing stop settings, or whatever your trading system demands.

Margin Check

MetaTrader comes with functions that allow you to check the current *free margin* or *stop out level* before placing an order. The stop out level is the percentage or amount of free margin below which you will not be able to place orders. Manually checking the free margin or stop out level before placing an order is not really necessary however, as an error will occur if you try to place an order with too little margin.

A more useful idea would be to determine your own stop out level, and halt trading if the current equity goes below that level. Let's start by declaring an external variable called `MinimumEquity`, which is the minimum amount of equity required in our account before we can place an order.

We'll compare `MinimumEquity` to our current account equity. If the current equity is less than our minimum equity, the order will not be placed, and an alert message will inform the user of the condition. Let's assume we have an account balance of $10,000. If we lose more than 20% of that equity, we do not want to place the order. Here is the code to check the minimum equity:

```
// External variables
extern int MinimumEquity = 8000;


// Order placement
if(AccountEquity() > MinimumEquity)
  {
    // Place order
  }
else if(AccountEquity() <= MinimumEquity)
  {
    Alert("Current equity is less than minimum equity! Order not placed.");
  }
```

The external variable `MinimumEquity` is placed at the beginning of the file. The rest of the code comes before and after the order placement function. If the current equity, as indicated by `AccountEquity()`, is greater than `MinimumEquity`, the order will be placed. Otherwise, the order will not be placed and an alert message will be displayed.

Spread Check

You may wish to avoid placing trades during periods where the spread has widened far beyond normal. We can set a maximum spread and check the current spread before trading. We'll declare an external variable called `MaximumSpread`, and use `MarketInfo()` to check the current spread.

The code will be very similar to the previous section where we added the minimum margin check. We will include the code from the previous section to show how these various checks work together:

```
// External variables
extern int MaximumSpread = 5;
extern int MinimumEquity = 8000;


if(AccountEquity() > MinimumEquity && MarketInfo(Symbol(),MODE_SPREAD) < MaximumSpread)
  {
    // Place order
  }
else
  {
    if(AccountEquity() <= MinimumEquity) Alert("Current equity is less than minimum
        equity! Order not placed.");

    if(MarketInfo(Symbol(),MODE_SPREAD) > MaximumSpread) Alert("Current spread is
        greater than maximum spread! Order not placed.");
  }
```

Note that we perform both the minimum equity check and the spread check before placing the order. If an one of the conditions are false, we go to the **else** block and check to see which of the conditions caused the order to not be placed. We will display one or more alerts depending on which condition is true.

Multiple Orders

You may wish to place multiple orders per position with different stop loss and take profit levels, as well as lot sizes. There are several ways to accomplish this. One way is to simply use a different **OrderSend()** statement for each order you want to place. This is assuming that you plan on placing the same number of orders every time.

Another way is to use a **for** loop to place the orders. This way, you can adjust the number of orders to place at one time. You can pre-load your stop loss and take profit prices into arrays, and increment through the arrays in the **for** loop.

Let's start by defining external variables for three stop loss and take profit levels. Any additional orders above three will not have a stop loss or take profit placed. We'll also add an external variable to adjust the number of orders to place.

```
extern int StopLoss1 = 20;
extern int StopLoss2 = 40;
extern int StopLoss3 = 60;
```

```
extern int TakeProfit1 = 40;
extern int TakeProfit2 = 80;
extern int TakeProfit3 = 120;

extern int MaxOrders = 3;
```

Next, we will declare our arrays, calculate our stop loss and take profit, and load our calculated prices into the array:

```
double BuyTakeProfit[3];
double BuyStopLoss[3];

BuyTakeProfit[0] = CalcBuyTakeProfit(Symbol(),TakeProfit1,Ask);
BuyTakeProfit[1] = CalcBuyTakeProfit(Symbol(),TakeProfit2,Ask);
BuyTakeProfit[2] = CalcBuyTakeProfit(Symbol(),TakeProfit3,Ask);

BuyStopLoss[0] = CalcBuyStopLoss(Symbol(),StopLoss1,Ask);
BuyStopLoss[1] = CalcBuyStopLoss(Symbol(),StopLoss2,Ask);
BuyStopLoss[2] = CalcBuyStopLoss(Symbol(),StopLoss3,Ask);
```

We start by declaring the arrays to hold the stop loss and take profit prices, **BuyTakeProfit** and **BuyStopLoss**. The number of array elements must be indicated when declaring the array. Array indexes start at zero, so by declaring an array dimension size of 3, our starting index is 0, and our largest index is 2.

Next, we calculate the stop loss and take profit prices using the functions we defined in chapter 4 – **CalcBuyStopLoss()** and **CalcBuyTakeProfit()**. We assign the calculated stop loss or take profit value to the appropriate array element. Note that the first array index is 0 and the third array index is 2.

Here is the **for** loop for placing the orders:

```
for(int Count = 0; Count <= MaxOrders - 1; Count++)
  {
    int OrdInt = Count + 1;

    OrderSend(Symbol(),OP_BUY,LotSize,Ask,UseSlippage,BuyStopLoss[Count],
      BuyTakeProfit[Count],"Buy Order "+OrdInt,MagicNumber,0,Green);
  }
```

The **Count** variable starts at 0, to correspond with our first array element. The number of times to loop (*i.e.* the number of orders to place) is determined by **MaxOrders - 1**. For each iteration of the loop, we increment the stop loss and take profit arrays by one.

We use the **OrdInt** variable to increment the order count in the order comment. The first order comment will be "Buy Order 1", the next will be "Buy Order 2" and so on. The **OrderSend()** function places the order with the appropriate stop loss and take profit value, using the **Count** variable to select the relevant array element.

This is just one way of handling multiple orders, although it is probably the most efficient. The main drawback to this approach is that we can only calculate stop loss and take profit prices for a limited number of orders. Alternately, we could scale the take profit and stop loss values by a specified amount, and place a potentially unlimited number of orders:

```
extern int StopLossStart = 20;
extern int StopLossIncr = 20;

extern int TakeProfitStart = 40;
extern int TakeProfitIncr = 40;

extern int MaxOrders = 5;
```

In the above example, the stop loss for our first order will be 20 pips. We will increment the stop loss by 20 pips for each additional order. Same for the take profit, except we will start at 40 and increment by 40. Instead of using arrays, we will calculate the stop loss and take profit in the **for** loop:

```
for(int Count = 0; Count <= MaxOrders - 1; Count++)
  {
     int OrdInt = Count + 1;

     int UseStopLoss =  StopLossStart + (StopLossIncr * Count);
     int UseTakeProfit =  TakeProfitStart + (TakeProfitIncr * Count);

     double BuyStopLoss = CalcBuyStopLoss(Symbol(),UseStopLoss,Ask);
     double BuyTakeProfit = CalcBuyTakeProfit(Symbol(),UseTakeProfit,Ask);

     OrderSend(Symbol(),OP_BUY,LotSize,Ask,UseSlippage,BuyStopLoss,
        BuyTakeProfit,"Buy Order "+OrdInt,MagicNumber,0,Green);
  }
```

We determine the take profit and stop loss level in pips by multiplying the **StopLossIncr** or **TakeProfitIncr** variable by the **Count**, and adding that to the **StopLossStart** or **TakeProfitStart** value. For the first order, the stop loss or take profit level will be equal to **StopLossStart** or **TakeProfitStart**.

Next, we calculate the stop loss and take profit price for the order using our functions from chapter 4. Finally we place the order using **OrderSend()**. The loop will continue until the number of orders specified by **MaxOrders** are placed. This method allows us to specify as many orders as we want using the **MaxOrders** variable, guaranteeing that every order we place will have a stop loss and a take profit.

Global Variables

In this book, we've been referring to variables with a global scope as "global variables." MetaTrader has a set of functions for setting variables at the terminal level, which means that these variables are available to every expert advisor that is currently running, assuming that we know the name of the variable to start with.

The MQL documentation refers to these as "global variables", although a more appropriate name might be "terminal variables." We use the global variable functions in the MQL Reference under *Global variables* to work with these types of variables. The current list of global variables in the terminal can be viewed by selecting *Global Variables* from the *Tools* menu, or by pressing F3 on the keyboard.

One way to use these variables is to store certain globally scoped or static variables to the terminal, so that if an expert advisor is shut down, we can pick up where we left off. Not all expert advisors require this, but more complex expert advisors will maintain a certain state that, if interrupted, will throw off the expert advisor's operation.

The best way to prevent this is to avoid creating expert advisors that require such a level of complexity. But if it can't be avoided, then using global variable functions to store the current state to the terminal may be helpful in case of accidental shutdown. Note that this method is not foolproof, but it is likely the best method to achieve this.

To declare a global (terminal) variable, use the **GlobalVariableSet()** function. The first argument is a string indicating the name of the global variable, and the second argument is a value of type double to assign to it.

```
GlobalVariableSet(GlobalVariableName,DoubleValue);
```

To keep your variable names unique, you may wish to create a global variable prefix. Declare a globally scoped variable in your expert advisor, and set the value in the **init()** function, using the current symbol, period, expert advisor name and magic number to create a unique variable prefix.

```
    // Global variables
    string GlobalVariablePrefix;

    int init()
      {
         GlobalVariablePrefix = Symbol()+Period()+"_"+"ProfitBuster"+"_"+MagicNumber+"_";
      }
```

We use the current symbol and period, along with an identifier for the EA and the `MagicNumber` external variable. Now, when we set a global variable using `GlobalVariableSet()`, we use the prefix that we defined above, along with the actual variable name:

```
    GlobalVariableSet(GlobalVariablePrefix+Counter,Counter);
```

So if we're trading on EURUSD on the M15 timeframe with an EA named "ProfitBuster", using 11 as our magic number and `Counter` as our variable name, the name of our global variable will be **EURUSD15_ProfitBuster_11_Counter**. You can use any convention you wish for naming your global variables, but including the above information is strongly recommended.

To retrieve the value of a global variable, use the function `GlobalVariableGet()` with the variable name as the argument:

```
    Counter = GlobalVariableGet(GlobalVariablePrefix+Counter);
```

To delete a global variable, use the function `GlobalVariableDel()` with the variable name as the argument. To delete all global variables placed by your EA, use the function `GlobalVariableDeleteAll()` with your prefix as the argument.

```
    GlobalVariableDel(GlobalVariablePrefix+Counter);
    GlobalVariableDeleteAll(GlobalVariablePrefix);
```

For more information on global variable functions, see the *Global variables* topic in the MQL Reference.

Check Order Profit

Sometimes it may be useful to check the current profit on an order, or to check the total profit on an order that has already closed. There are two ways to check profit. To get the profit in the deposit currency, use the `OrderProfit()` function. You must first select the order using `OrderSelect()`.

```
OrderSelect(Ticket,SELECT_BY_TICKET);
double GetProfit = OrderProfit(Ticket);
```

The result of the **OrderProfit()** function should be identical to the total profit or loss that is listed in the order history for the selected order.

To retrieve the profit or loss in pips, you will need to calculate the difference between the order opening price and the order closing price. You will also need to use the **OrderSelect()** function to retrieve the open and close prices.

```
OrderSelect(Ticket,SELECT_BY_TICKET);

if(OrderType() == OP_BUY) double GetProfit = OrderClosePrice() - OrderOpenPrice();
else if(OrderType() == OP_SELL) GetProfit = OrderOpenPrice() - OrderClosePrice();

GetProfit /= PipPoint(Symbol());
```

For buy orders, we calculate the profit by subtracting the opening price from the closing price. For sell orders, we do the opposite. After we've calculated the difference, we can convert the profit or loss to a whole number by dividing it by the point, using our **PipPoint()** function.

For example, if our buy order opening price is 1.4650 and our closing price is 1.4700, the difference between **OrderClosePrice()** and **OrderOpenPrice()** is 0.0050. When we divide that by our **PipPoint()** function, the result is 50. So for this order, we make 50 pips in profit. If the order closing price was 1.4600 instead, then we'd have a loss of -50 pips.

Martingale

Martingale is a betting system, commonly used in roulette and blackjack, where the bet size is doubled after each consecutive loss. The theory is that one winning bet will bring the balance back to break even. The downside to Martingale is that you need a lot of capital to withstand the drawdowns.

For example, if your starting lot size is 0.1 lots, after 4 consecutive losses your lot size will be 1.6 lots – 16 times your original lot size. After 7 consecutive losses, your lot size will be 12.8 lots – 128 times your original lot size! A long losing streak will wipe out your account before you'll be able to bring your account back to break even.

Nevertheless, you may wish to incorporate a system of increasing lot sizes on consecutive wins or losses, and it's possible to do so without wiping out your account. The easiest method is to put a cap on the number of times to increase the lot size. A sound trading system should not have more than 3 or 4 maximum consecutive losses. You can determine this by examining the maximum consecutive loss count under the *Report* tab in the Strategy Tester window.

Another method is to increase your lot size by a smaller multiplier. The classic Martingale strategy doubles the lot size after each consecutive loss. You may wish to use a multiplier smaller than 2. There is also the anti-Martingale strategy, where you increase the lot size after each consecutive win.

Let's examine a routine where we calculate the number of consecutive wins or losses, and increase the lot size accordingly. A Martingale strategy works best when you're placing one order at a time, so we will assume that every position consists of a single trade.

The user will be able to choose between a Martingale (losses) or anti-Martingale (wins) strategy. A setting to limit the maximum number of consecutive lot increases will be included, and the lot multiplier will be adjustable.

First, let's calculate the number of consecutive wins or losses. We will need to loop through the order history pool backward, starting from the most recently closed order. We will increment a counter for each win or loss. As long as a pattern of consecutive wins or losses is maintained, we will continue to loop. As soon as the pattern is broken (a win is located after one or more losses, or vice versa), the loop will exit.

```
int WinCount;
int LossCount;

for(int Count = OrdersHistoryTotal()-1; ; Count--)
   {
     OrderSelect(Count,SELECT_BY_POS,MODE_HISTORY);
     if(OrderSymbol() == Symbol() && OrderMagicNumber() == MagicNumber)
        {
          if(OrderProfit() > 0 && LossCount == 0) WinCount++;
          else if(OrderProfit() < 0 && WinCount == 0) LossCount++;
          else break;
        }
   }
```

We start by declaring the variables for our win and loss counters. In the **for** operator, notice that we use **OrdersHistoryTotal()** to establish our initial starting position. **OrdersHistoryTotal()** returns the number of orders in the history pool. We subtract 1 to determine the index position for the most recent order, which is stored in the **Count** variable.

Notice that we have omitted the second expression in the **for** loop – the one that determines the condition to stop looping. The semicolon must remain for any omitted expressions. We will decrement the **Count** variable on each iteration of the loop.

We use **MODE_HISTORY** as the third argument in the **OrderSelect()** function to indicate that we are looping through the closed order history pool. By default, **OrderSelect()** uses the open order pool, so we must specify **MODE_HISTORY** when checking the closed order pool.

We check to make sure that the currently selected order matches our chart symbol and our magic number. Then, we examine the order profit using the **OrderProfit()** function. If the return value indicates a profit (*i.e.* is greater than zero), then we increment the **WinCount** variable. If it's a loss, we increment **LossCount**.

Since we are looking for consecutive wins or losses, we need to terminate the loop once an alternating condition is found. To do this, we check the **WinCount** or **LossCount** variable when checking the order profit. For example, if we have 2 consecutive losses – meaning that **LossCount** = 2 – and our next order is a win, then both of our **if** statements will be false, and control will pass to the **break** operator, which ends the loop.

The advantage of this method is that it's robust, and will not fail if the expert advisor is accidentally shut down. The EA will pick up right where it left off. Of course, this means that when you first start the EA, it will use any previous win/loss streak when determining the lot size. But as you can see, the advantages outweigh the disadvantages.

Either the **WinCount** or the **LossCount** variable will contain the number of consecutive wins or losses. If we want to do a Martingale strategy, we use **LossCount** to determine the factor by which to increase the lot size. If we're doing an anti-Martingale, we use **WinCount** instead.

We'll use an external integer variable called **MartingaleType** to determine this. If **MartingaleType** is set to 0, we'll use the Martingale strategy. If it's set to 1, we'll use the anti-Martingale strategy. We will also declare external variables for our multiplier (**LotMultiplier**), the maximum number of times to increase the lot size (**MaxMartingale**), and our starting lot size (**BaseLotSize**).

```
// External variables
extern int MartingaleType = 0;       // 0: Martingale, 1: Anti-Martingale
extern int LotMultiplier = 2;
extern int MaxMartingale = 4;
extern double BaseLotSize = 0.1;


// Lot size calculation
if(MartingaleType == 0) int ConsecutiveCount = LossCount;
else if(MartingaleType = 1) ConsecutiveCount = WinCount;

if(ConsecutiveCount > MaxMartingale) ConsecutiveCount = MaxMartingale;

double LotSize = BaseLotSize * MathPow(LotMultiplier,ConsecutiveCount);
```

We set the value of **ConsecutiveCount** to either **WinCount** or **LossCount**, depending on the **MartingaleType** setting. We'll compare that to our **MaxMartingale** setting. If our consecutive order count is greater than **MaxMartingale**, we will resize it to be equal to **MaxMartingale**. (You could also resize it to the default lot size if you prefer.) The lot size will remain at this size until a win or loss breaks our consecutive order streak.

The lot size is determined by multiplying our **BaseLotSize** by the **LotMultiplier**, which is exponentially increased by **ConsecutiveCount**. The **MathPow()** function raises a number to the specified power. The first argument is the base, and the second argument is the exponent. For example, if our starting lot size is 0.1, the lot multiplier is 2, and we have four consecutive orders, the equation is $\mathtt{0.1\ *\ 2^4\ =\ 1.6}$.

By adjusting the **LotMultiplier** and using both Martingale and anti-Martingale strategies, this will give you enough options to experiment with using exponential lot sizing. You can easily modify the code above to use other variations. For example, you could scale lot sizes in reverse, from largest to smallest. Or you could use an external counter in place of **ConsecutiveCount**.

Debugging Your Expert Advisor

Unlike most programming IDEs, MetaEditor doesn't support breakpoints or any other kind of modern debugging techniques. You'll need to use **Print()** statements and logs to debug your expert advisors.

You've already been introduced to the **Print()** function. In summary, any string argument passed to the function will be printed to the log. By printing the contents of variables and functions to the log, you can examine the output of your code and fix any errors.

You'll want to use the Strategy Tester to run a trading simulation and examine the log output. The Strategy Tester log is displayed under the *Journal* tab in the Strategy Tester window. There is a limit to the amount of information that is listed in the Journal tab, so you may want to view the actual log.

The Strategy Tester logs are stored in the **\tester\logs** folder. Right click anywhere in the Journal window and select *Open* from the pop-up menu. A Windows Explorer window will open, displaying the contents of the log folder. The file names are in the format **yyyymmdd.log**, where **yyyy** is the four digit year, **mm** is the two digit month, and **dd** is the two digit date. You can view the logs in Notepad or any text editor.

Let's illustrate an example of how you can use the log to locate a programming problem. The code below has an error in it, and it is not performing as we expected. To be able to diagnose the problem, we need to check the input or output of the function. Let's create a `Print()` statement and print the contents of all relevant variables to the log.

We'll run the EA in the Strategy Tester, using *Open prices only* as our testing model. Make sure you're testing the EA over a long enough time period so that it will place enough trades for us to analyze. If you need to check prices on the chart, hit the *Open Chart* button to open a chart showing the simulated trades.

Next, we'll go to the Journal tab and check for the information we need. If we need to view the log in it's entirety, or if there are trades that are not showing in the Journal tab, we can right-click and choose Open from the pop-up menu, and open the log file directly.

This code is giving us error 130: "invalid stops" every time we place a buy order. We know that error 130 means that either the stop loss or the take profit is incorrect. Can you identify the error?

```
if(Close[0] > MA && BuyTicket == 0)
  {
    double OpenPrice = Ask;

    double BuyStopLoss = OpenPrice + (StopLoss * UsePoint);
    double BuyTakeProfit = OpenPrice + (TakeProfit * UsePoint);

    BuyTicket = OrderSend(Symbol(),OP_BUY,LotSize,OpenPrice,UseSlippage,
      BuyStopLoss,BuyTakeProfit,"Buy Order",MagicNumber,0,Green);

    SellTicket = 0;
  }
```

We will use the `Print()` function to verify the parameters that are being passed to the `OrderSend()` function. We'll focus on the order opening price, the stop loss and the take profit.

```
Print("Price:"+OpenPrice+" Stop:"+BuyStopLoss+" Profit:"+BuyTakeProfit);
```

Here is the output when we run the EA in the strategy tester. A stop loss and take profit of 50 pips is assumed:

```
11:52:12 2009.11.02 02:00  Example EURUSD,H1: OrderSend error 130
11:52:12 2009.11.02 02:00  Example EURUSD,H1: Price:1.47340000 Stop:1.47840000
  Profit:1.47840000
```

We know that the stop loss must be below the opening price for a buy order. Here, it is above the price. In fact, it's the same price as the take profit. A quick look at our code and we realize that we accidentally inserted a plus sign in the buy stop loss equation. Here is the correct code:

```
double BuyStopLoss = OpenPrice - (StopLoss * UsePoint);
```

If you are receiving an error message when attempting to place, close or modify an order, focus your efforts on the issue indicated by the error message. Here are a couple of the most common error messages cause by programming errors:

- **Error 129: Invalid Price** – The opening price is invalid. For market orders, make sure the current Bid or Ask price is being passed, according to the order type. For pending orders, make sure the price is above or below the current price, as required by the order type. Also check to see that the pending order price is not too close to the current price (*i.e.* inside the stop level).

- **Error 130: Invalid Stops** – Either the stop loss or take profit price is incorrect. Check to see that the stop loss and take profit prices are placed above or below the current price, depending on whether the order type is buy or sell. Also check to see that the stop loss or take profit price is not too close to the current price (*i.e.* inside the stop level).

- **Error 131: Invalid Trade Volume** – The lot size is incorrect. Make sure that the lot size does not exceed the broker minimum or maximum, and that the lot size is normalized to the correct step value (0.1 or 0.01 on most brokers).

Descriptions of all error messages can be found in the MQL Reference under *Standard Constants – Error Codes*. If you need additional assistance with an error that you are receiving, check the forums at MQL4.com.

Troubleshooting Intermittent Trading Errors

While most serious bugs can be found simply by back testing, others will occur only during real-time trading. Errors of logic can result in trades not being placed correctly, and these bugs can take some effort to locate. If there are trades being placed incorrectly during demo or live trading, we need as much information as necessary to troubleshoot the problem.

We're going to add an optional feature to log trade and status information in real-time, so that we have a record of it when troubleshooting trades. We'll be using **Print()** statements as previously, but we'll be logging indicator values, prices – any information that will be helpful in debugging. We'll also add an external variable to turn logging on and off.

```
// External variables
extern bool Debug = true;
```

```
// Place near the end of the start() function
if(Debug == true) Print(StringConcatenate("Bid:",Bid," Ask:",Ask," MA:",MA,
   " BuyTicket:",BuyTicket," SellTicket:",SellTicket));
```

The above code will log price and indicator information, as well as the contents of the **BuyTicket** and **SellTicket** variables. If there are any questions about how a trade was opened, or why a trade was not opened, the log at that particular moment will show the status of all relevant trade conditions. You can turn logging on and off with the **Debug** external variable.

The debug **Print()** statement should be placed near the end of the **start()** function, after all trading functions. If you are using a timer and/or an execute at bar open feature, place the debug **Print()** statement inside the timer block so that it will only run when necessary. Otherwise, the debug line will print to the log on every tick, which can result in a large log file.

Fixing Compilation Errors

When you compile your expert advisor, the compiler will check for correct syntax, and ensure that all custom functions and variables have been properly declared. If you've left something out, the compiler will stop, and any compilation errors will appear in the *Errors* tab in the *Toolbox* window.

When confronted with a long list of compilation errors, always start with the first one. Double-click the error in the list, and the editor will jump directly to the line with the error. Correct the error and recompile. Sometimes a simple syntax error will result in several unrelated errors, although only the first one was valid.

Here is a list of common compilation errors and their solutions:

- **Variable not defined** – You forgot to declare a variable with a data type. If it is a global or external variable, declare it at the top of the file. If it is a local variable, find the first occurrence and place the data type declaration in front of it. Otherwise, check the spelling or the case (upper/lower) of the variable name.

- **Variable already defined** – You declared the same variable twice. Remove the data type declaration from all duplicate variable declarations.

- **Function is not defined** – If the function in question is in an include or library file, be sure that the **#include** or **#import** directive is placed at the top of the file and is correct. Otherwise, check the spelling or the case of the function name, and be sure that it exists either in the current file or in the relevant include or library files.

- **Illegal assignment used** – This is usually in reference to an equal sign (=). Remember that a single equal sign is for variable assignment, and two equal signs (==) is a comparison operator. Correct the assignment operator to the appropriate comparison operator.

- **Assignment expected** – This is usually in reference to the "equal to" comparison operator (==). You used two equal signs instead of one in a variable assignment. Correct the operator to a single equal sign.

- **Unbalanced right parenthesis** – These usually occur in an `if` statement when using nested parentheses. Go to the line indicated by the first error and insert a left parenthesis in the appropriate place.

- **Unbalanced left parenthesis** – This is a tricky one. The error usually points to the end of program line. Basically you forgot a right parenthesis somewhere. Double check the code you recently edited and look for a missing right parenthesis. You may have to comment out lines of code to locate the problem.

- **Wrong parameters count** – You have too few or too many arguments in a function. Double check the function syntax in the MQL Reference and correct the arguments.

- **Semicolon expected** – You probably forgot to put a semicolon at the end of a line. Place a semicolon at the end of the previous line. Note that a missing semi-colon may cause any of the above errors as well, so be sure to place those semicolons!

Chapter 9
Custom Indicators and Scripts

No book on MQL would be complete without covering custom indicators and scripts. The built-in indicators in MetaTrader are rather limited, but fortunately MQL allows programmers to create their own indicators. If you're looking for a popular indicator that is not included in MT4, chances are someone has already created one.

This chapter will be a basic overview of custom indicator creation. Most indicators use complex mathematical formulas, and as such are the domain of more experienced programmers. However, an indicator need not be complex. We'll create a custom indicator in this chapter that uses only a few lines of code.

Buffers

Buffers are arrays that store indicator values and calculations. A custom indicator can have up to 8 buffers. Buffers use indexes, just like arrays do, and range from 0 to 7. When you call a custom indicator in an expert advisor using the `iCustom()` function, the next-to-last parameter in the function is the indicator buffer.

To find the appropriate buffer for an indicator line, you usually check the source code, if available. If the source code is clearly formatted with descriptive variable names, you should be able to identify the appropriate buffer quite easily. We will address the proper naming of indicator buffers in this chapter.

Creating A Custom Indicator

Let's build a custom indicator using two built-in MetaTrader indicators to calculate our lines. We're going to build a modified Bollinger Bands indicator. The Bollinger Bands consist of 3 lines – a center line which is a simple moving average, along with an upper and lower line whose value is determined by the standard deviation.

We can create our own Bollinger Bands indicator using the Moving Average and the Standard Deviation indicators. We'd like to create an indicator that uses an exponential moving average to calculate the lines, as opposed to a simple moving average.

146

We start by using the wizard to create our indicator file. Select *New* from the File menu or the toolbar to open the wizard, and create a custom indicator. Fill out the indicator name, and add parameters if you wish. On the final page, we added three indicator lines of the same color. Here is the result of the wizard. We've left out the **start()** function for now:

```
//+------------------------------------------------------------------+
//|                                               EMA Bollinger.mq4 |
//|                                                   Andrew Young |
//|                                      http://www.easyexpertforex.com |
//+------------------------------------------------------------------+
#property copyright "Andrew Young"
#property link      "http://www.easyexpertforex.com"

#property indicator_chart_window
#property indicator_buffers 3
#property indicator_color1 DeepSkyBlue
#property indicator_color2 DeepSkyBlue
#property indicator_color3 DeepSkyBlue
//---- buffers
double ExtMapBuffer1[];
double ExtMapBuffer2[];
double ExtMapBuffer3[];
//+------------------------------------------------------------------+
//| Custom indicator initialization function                         |
//+------------------------------------------------------------------+
int init()
  {
//---- indicators
   SetIndexStyle(0,DRAW_LINE);
   SetIndexBuffer(0,ExtMapBuffer1);
   SetIndexStyle(1,DRAW_LINE);
   SetIndexBuffer(1,ExtMapBuffer2);
   SetIndexStyle(2,DRAW_LINE);
   SetIndexBuffer(2,ExtMapBuffer3);
//----
   return(0);
  }
```

Let's turn our attention to the elements listed in bold. The **#property** declarations set the parameters for our indicator buffers. The **indicator_chart_window** property draws our indicator in the main chart window. If we were creating an oscillator, and wanted to draw the indicator in a separate window, we'd use the **indicator_separate_window** property instead.

The **indicator_buffers** property set the number of buffers for our indicator. In this case we are using three buffers. The **indicator_color** properties set the color of all three lines to **DeepSkyBlue**.

Next are the declarations for our buffer arrays. We have three buffers named **ExtMapBuffer*(1-3)***. We will change these array identifiers to something more descriptive shortly.

The **init()** function is where we set the properties for our indicator buffers. **SetIndexBuffer()** binds a buffer array to a buffer index. The buffer index is what we refer to when we set the properties for an indicator line, and also when we call an indicator line from an EA using the **iCustom()** function. The first parameter is an integer from 0 to 7, and the second parameter is the name of the buffer array.

Drawing Properties

The **SetIndexStyle()** function sets the type of line to draw, along with the properties of that line. Every indicator line will have a corresponding **SetIndexStyle()** function. Here is the syntax:

```
void SetIndexStyle(int BufferIndex, int LineType, int LineStyle = EMPTY,
    int LineWidth = EMPTY, color LineColor = CLR_NONE)
```

- **BufferIndex** – The index of the buffer, from 0 to 7.

- **LineType** – Sets the type of line to draw. **DRAW_LINE** draws a single line, **DRAW_HISTOGRAM** draws a vertical histogram (see the OsMA or Awesome Oscillator indicators for examples), **DRAW_ARROW** draws a symbol, and **DRAW_NONE** draws no line.

- **LineStyle** – An optional parameter indicating the drawing style. Used mainly for lines of type **DRAW_LINE**. By default, a solid line is drawn (**STYLE_SOLID**). You can also draw dashed (**STYLE_DASH**) and dotted (**STYLE_DOT**) lines.

- **LineWidth** – An optional parameter indicating the width of the line in pixels. The default value is 1.

- **LineColor** – An optional parameter indicating the color of the line. If you use the wizard, the color is set using **#property** declarations, but you can set the color here as well.

If you are using **DRAW_ARROW** as the **LineType**, the **SetArrow()** function allows you to set the Wingdings font symbol to draw on the chart. The first parameter is the buffer index, and the second is an integer constant representing the symbol to draw. The symbols can be found in the MQL Reference under *Standard Constants – Arrow Codes*.

You may want to add a description for the indicator lines that will be displayed in the tooltip or in the data window. To do this, use the **SetIndexLabel()** function. The first parameter is the buffer index, and the second parameter is a text description. We'll add these to our indicator shortly.

If your indicator is drawn in a separate window (such as an oscillator), and you'd like to add levels to indicate overbought or oversold levels (such as in the Stochastic or RSI indicators), or the zero level (such as in the CCI indicator), you can use the **SetLevelStyle()** and **SetLevelValue()** functions. See the MQL Reference under *Custom Indicators* for more information.

You may also want to specify a short indicator name to be displayed in the top left corner of the indicator window. Use the **IndicatorShortName()** function to set this value. The only parameter is a text string that will appear in the top left corner of the indicator window, as well as in the data window.

Using Descriptive Buffer Names

Here is our updated indicator code. Note that we've renamed the buffer arrays to be more descriptive as to their actual function. We've changed the second parameter of the **SetIndexBuffer()** functions to reflect the new buffer names. We've also added **SetIndexLabel()** for each line to display descriptive names in the Data Window.

```
//---- buffers
double EMA[];
double UpperBand[];
double LowerBand[];
//+------------------------------------------------------------------+
//| Custom indicator initialization function                         |
//+------------------------------------------------------------------+
int init()
  {
//---- indicators
   SetIndexStyle(0,DRAW_LINE);
   SetIndexBuffer(0,EMA);
   SetIndexLabel(0,"EMA");

   SetIndexStyle(1,DRAW_LINE);
   SetIndexBuffer(1,UpperBand);
   SetIndexLabel(1,"UpperBand");

   SetIndexStyle(2,DRAW_LINE);
   SetIndexBuffer(2,LowerBand);
   SetIndexLabel(2,"LowerBand");
//----
   return(0);
  }
```

We've renamed our buffer arrays from the default names (**ExtMapBuffer**) to more descriptive ones. **EMA[]** will be our buffer for the center line, and **UpperBand[]** and **LowerBand[]** will be the upper and lower bands respectively.

The **SetIndexBuffer()** functions bind the buffer indexes to our buffer arrays. **EMA** is 0, **UpperBand** is 1, and **LowerBand** is 2. Note that the braces are left out of the array identifier name for the second **SetIndexBuffer()** parameter.

The **SetIndexLabel()** functions set a descriptive name for each of the indicator buffers. In this case, the line names are the same as our identifier names. These will appear on the mouse tooltip as well as in the Data Window. If another programmer decides to use this indicator in an expert advisor, the formatting above will make it clear exactly which indicator buffer index they should use for each line.

The Indicator start() Function

The wizard inserts just one expression in the **start()** function:

```
int counted_bars = IndicatorCounted();
```

IndicatorCounted() returns the number of bars on the chart that the indicator has already calculated. When the EA is first started, this value will be 0. The indicator will be calculated for every bar on the chart. On subsequent bars, we will check the **IndicatorCounted()** function to see how many bars have already been calculated, so we'll know exactly how many new bars we'll need to calculate.

Our indicator calculations will occur inside a **for** loop. The starting point will be the first uncalculated bar, and the end point will be the current bar. We'll compare the value of **IndicatorCounted()** to the predefined **Bars** variable, which returns the number of bars on the current chart. This will determine our starting point. Here is the code for the **for** loop:

```
int counted_bars = IndicatorCounted();

if(counted_bars > 0) counted_bars--;

int CalculateBars = Bars - counted_bars;

for(int Count = CalculateBars; Count >= 0; Count--)
  {
    // Indicator calculations
  }
```

The first **if** statement will decrement the value of **counted_bars** by 1 when calculating new bars. We will always be calculating at least the two previous bars. This is due to a condition where the final tick of a bar may not be calculated in some cases. Next, we determine the number of bars to calculate, by subtracting **counted_bars** from the predefined **Bars** variable. This is stored in the variable **CalculateBars**.

In our **for** loop, the incrementing variable **Count** is set to the value of **CalculateBars**, the condition for termination is when **Count** is less than 0, and the **Count** variable is decremented on each iteration. This will calculate each bar on the chart from left to right.

Here is the code to calculate our Bollinger Bands. We'll declare the external variable **BandsPeriod** at the beginning of the file. The **for** loop is the one we created above:

```
// External parameters
extern int BandsPeriod = 20;


// start() function
for(int Count = CalculateBars; Count >= 0; Count--)
  {
    EMA[Count] = iMA(NULL,0,BandsPeriod,0,MODE_EMA,0,Count);

    double StdDev = iStdDev(NULL,0,BandsPeriod,0,MODE_EMA,0,Count);

    UpperBand[Count] = EMA[Count] + StdDev;
    LowerBand[Count] = EMA[Count] - StdDev;
  }
```

First, we call the built-in Moving Average indicator using the **iMA()** function, and assign the return value to **EMA[Count]**. Note that the array index and the **Shift** parameter for the moving average indicator both use the current **Count** value.

Next, we call the Standard Deviation indicator using **iStdDev()**. To calculate the upper band, all we need to do is add the standard deviation to the moving average line. This is stored in the buffer array **UpperBand[]**. To calculate **LowerBand[]**, we subtract the standard deviation from the moving average.

Let's extend our indicator a bit more by giving it a full range of settings. We'll add settings to adjust the forward shift, moving average method, and applied price parameters, as well as a standard deviation adjustment:

```
// External parameters
extern int BandsPeriod = 20;
extern int BandsShift = 0;
extern int BandsMethod = 1;
extern int BandsPrice = 0;
extern int Deviations = 1;
```

```
// start() function
for(int Count = CalculateBars; Count >= 0; Count--)
  {
     EMA[Count] = iMA(NULL,0,BandsPeriod,BandsShift,BandsMethod,BandsPrice,Count);

     double StdDev = iStdDev(NULL,0,BandsPeriod,BandsShift,BandsMethod,BandsPrice,Count);

     UpperBand[Count] = EMA[Count] + (StdDev * Deviations);
     LowerBand[Count] = EMA[Count] - (StdDev * Deviations);
  }
```

We've added external variables to adjust the remaining parameters for the **iMA()** and **iStdDev()** functions. We also added a parameter to adjust the number of standard deviations. To calculate this, we simply multiply **StdDev** by **Deviations**. Now we have a fully adjustable Bollinger Bands indicator that is more flexible than the standard MetaTrader indicator. The full code is listed in Appendix E.

You can do more with custom indicators than just recalculate built-in indicators. Depending on your level of mathematical knowledge, you can code indicators that aren't included with MetaTrader, or even create your own. You can also draw and manipulate objects as well. If you'd like to learn more about custom indicator creation, see the MQL Reference topics *Custom indicators, Object functions* and *Math & Trig.*

Scripts

A script is an MQL program that runs only once, when it is first attached to a chart. Scripts can be used to automate a series of trading actions, such as closing all orders on the chart or sending a pending order. Some scripts, such as the **period_converter** script that ships with MetaTrader, can redraw the chart based on a custom time period.

A script source code file should have either the **show_confirm** or **show_inputs** property directive. The **show_confirm** property prompts the user to confirm the operation of the script, while **show_inputs** displays the script properties dialog.

```
#property show_confirm    // shows confirm dialog
#property show_inputs     // shows properties dialog
```

If your script has parameters that need to be adjusted, use the **show_inputs** property. Otherwise, use **show_confirm**.

Just like expert advisors and indicators, scripts use the `init()`, `deinit()` and `start()` functions. Remember that each function will only be run once – `init()` and `start()` when the script is started, and `deinit()` when it is removed. You can have one script attached to a chart at a time.

MetaTrader comes with several sample scripts. All scripts are saved in the `\experts\scripts` directory.

Appendix A

Simple Expert Advisor

This is the simple expert advisor from chapter 2.

```
#property copyright "Andrew Young"


// External variables
extern double LotSize = 0.1;
extern double StopLoss = 50;
extern double TakeProfit = 100;

extern int Slippage = 5;
extern int MagicNumber = 123;

extern int FastMAPeriod = 10;
extern int SlowMAPeriod = 20;


// Global variables
int BuyTicket;
int SellTicket;
double UsePoint;
int UseSlippage;


// Init function
int init()
  {
    UsePoint = PipPoint(Symbol());
    UseSlippage = GetSlippage(Symbol(),Slippage);
  }


// Start function
int start()
  {

    // Moving averages
    double FastMA = iMA(NULL,0,FastMAPeriod,0,0,0,0);
    double SlowMA = iMA(NULL,0,SlowMAPeriod,0,0,0,0);
```

```
// Buy order
if(FastMA > SlowMA && BuyTicket == 0)
  {
    OrderSelect(SellTicket,SELECT_BY_TICKET);

    // Close order
    if(OrderCloseTime() == 0 && SellTicket > 0)
      {
        double CloseLots = OrderLots();
        double ClosePrice = Ask;

        bool Closed = OrderClose(SellTicket,CloseLots,ClosePrice,UseSlippage,Red);
      }

    double OpenPrice = Ask;

    // Calculate stop loss and take profit
    if(StopLoss > 0) double BuyStopLoss = OpenPrice - (StopLoss * UsePoint);
    if(TakeProfit > 0) double BuyTakeProfit = OpenPrice + (TakeProfit * UsePoint);

    // Open buy order
    BuyTicket = OrderSend(Symbol(),OP_BUY,LotSize,OpenPrice,UseSlippage,
      BuyStopLoss,BuyTakeProfit,"Buy Order",MagicNumber,0,Green);

    SellTicket = 0;
  }


// Sell Order
if(FastMA < SlowMA && SellTicket == 0)
  {
    OrderSelect(BuyTicket,SELECT_BY_TICKET);

    if(OrderCloseTime() == 0 && BuyTicket > 0)
      {
        CloseLots = OrderLots();
        ClosePrice = Bid;

        Closed = OrderClose(BuyTicket,CloseLots,ClosePrice,UseSlippage,Red);
      }

    OpenPrice = Bid;

    if(StopLoss > 0) double SellStopLoss = OpenPrice + (StopLoss * UsePoint);
    if(TakeProfit > 0) double SellTakeProfit = OpenPrice - (TakeProfit * UsePoint);

    SellTicket = OrderSend(Symbol(),OP_SELL,LotSize,OpenPrice,UseSlippage,
      SellStopLoss,SellTakeProfit,"Sell Order",MagicNumber,0,Red);

    BuyTicket = 0;
  }
```

```
        return(0);
    }


// Pip Point Function
double PipPoint(string Currency)
    {
      int CalcDigits = MarketInfo(Currency,MODE_DIGITS);
      if(CalcDigits == 2 || CalcDigits == 3) double CalcPoint = 0.01;
      else if(CalcDigits == 4 || CalcDigits == 5) CalcPoint = 0.0001;
      return(CalcPoint);
    }


// Get Slippage Function
int GetSlippage(string Currency, int SlippagePips)
    {
      int CalcDigits = MarketInfo(Currency,MODE_DIGITS);
      if(CalcDigits == 2 || CalcDigits == 4) double CalcSlippage = SlippagePips;
      else if(CalcDigits == 3 || CalcDigits == 5) CalcSlippage = SlippagePips * 10;
      return(CalcSlippage);
    }
```

Simple Expert Advisor with Pending Orders

Here is the simple expert advisor using pending stop orders:

```
#property copyright "Andrew Young"


// External variables
extern double LotSize = 0.1;
extern double StopLoss = 50;
extern double TakeProfit = 100;
extern int PendingPips = 10;

extern int Slippage = 5;
extern int MagicNumber = 123;

extern int FastMAPeriod = 10;
extern int SlowMAPeriod = 20;


// Global variables
int BuyTicket;
int SellTicket;
double UsePoint;
int UseSlippage;
```

```
// Init function
int init()
  {
    UsePoint = PipPoint(Symbol());
    UseSlippage = GetSlippage(Symbol(),Slippage);
  }


// Start function
int start()
  {

    // Moving averages
    double FastMA = iMA(NULL,0,FastMAPeriod,0,0,0,0);
    double SlowMA = iMA(NULL,0,SlowMAPeriod,0,0,0,0);


    // Buy order
    if(FastMA > SlowMA && BuyTicket == 0)
      {
        OrderSelect(SellTicket,SELECT_BY_TICKET);

        // Close order
        if(OrderCloseTime() == 0 && SellTicket > 0 && OrderType() == OP_SELL)
          {
            double CloseLots = OrderLots();
            double ClosePrice = Ask;

            bool Closed = OrderClose(SellTicket,CloseLots,ClosePrice,UseSlippage,Red);
          }

        // Delete Order
        else if(OrderCloseTime() == 0 && SellTicket > 0 && OrderType() == OP_SELLSTOP)
          {
            bool Deleted = OrderDelete(SellTicket,Red);
          }

        double PendingPrice = High[0] + (PendingPips * UsePoint);

        // Calculate stop loss and take profit
        if(StopLoss > 0) double BuyStopLoss = PendingPrice - (StopLoss * UsePoint);
        if(TakeProfit > 0) double BuyTakeProfit = PendingPrice +
          (TakeProfit * UsePoint);

        // Open buy order
        BuyTicket = OrderSend(Symbol(),OP_BUYSTOP,LotSize,PendingPrice,UseSlippage,
          BuyStopLoss,BuyTakeProfit,"Buy Stop Order",MagicNumber,0,Green);

        SellTicket = 0;
      }
```

```
    // Sell Order
    if(FastMA < SlowMA && SellTicket == 0)
      {
        OrderSelect(BuyTicket,SELECT_BY_TICKET);

        if(OrderCloseTime() == 0 && BuyTicket > 0 && OrderType() == OP_BUY)
          {
            CloseLots = OrderLots();
            ClosePrice = Bid;

            Closed = OrderClose(BuyTicket,CloseLots,ClosePrice,UseSlippage,Red);
          }

        else if(OrderCloseTime() == 0 && SellTicket > 0 && OrderType() == OP_BUYSTOP)
          {
            Deleted = OrderDelete(SellTicket,Red);
          }

        PendingPrice = Low[0] - (PendingPips * UsePoint);

        if(StopLoss > 0) double SellStopLoss = PendingPrice + (StopLoss * UsePoint);
        if(TakeProfit > 0) double SellTakeProfit = PendingPrice -
          (TakeProfit * UsePoint);

        SellTicket = OrderSend(Symbol(),OP_SELLSTOP,LotSize,PendingPrice,UseSlippage,
          SellStopLoss,SellTakeProfit,"Sell Stop Order",MagicNumber,0,Red);

        BuyTicket = 0;
      }

    return(0);
  }


// Pip Point Function
double PipPoint(string Currency)
  {
    int CalcDigits = MarketInfo(Currency,MODE_DIGITS);
    if(CalcDigits == 2 || CalcDigits == 3) double CalcPoint = 0.01;
    else if(CalcDigits == 4 || CalcDigits == 5) CalcPoint = 0.0001;
    return(CalcPoint);
  }


// Get Slippage Function
int GetSlippage(string Currency, int SlippagePips)
  {
    int CalcDigits = MarketInfo(Currency,MODE_DIGITS);
    if(CalcDigits == 2 || CalcDigits == 4) double CalcSlippage = SlippagePips;
    else if(CalcDigits == 3 || CalcDigits == 5) CalcSlippage = SlippagePips * 10;
    return(CalcSlippage);
  }
```

Appendix B

Advanced Expert Advisor

This is the expert advisor with advanced features from chapter 3.

```
#property copyright "Andrew Young"
#include <stdlib.mqh>


// External variables
extern bool DynamicLotSize = true;
extern double EquityPercent = 2;
extern double FixedLotSize = 0.1;
extern double StopLoss = 50;
extern double TakeProfit = 100;
extern int Slippage = 5;
extern int MagicNumber = 123;
extern int FastMAPeriod = 10;
extern int SlowMAPeriod = 20;


// Global variables
int BuyTicket;
int SellTicket;

double UsePoint;
int UseSlippage;

int ErrorCode;


// Init function
int init()
  {
    UsePoint = PipPoint(Symbol());
    UseSlippage = GetSlippage(Symbol(),Slippage);
  }


// Start function
int start()
  {

    // Moving averages
    double FastMA = iMA(NULL,0,FastMAPeriod,0,0,0,1);
    double SlowMA = iMA(NULL,0,SlowMAPeriod,0,0,0,1);
```

```
// Lot size calculation
if(DynamicLotSize == true)
  {
     double RiskAmount = AccountEquity() * (EquityPercent / 100);
     double TickValue = MarketInfo(Symbol(),MODE_TICKVALUE);
     if(Point == 0.001 || Point == 0.00001) TickValue *= 10;
     double CalcLots = (RiskAmount / StopLoss) / TickValue;
     double LotSize = CalcLots;
  }
else LotSize = FixedLotSize;


// Lot size verification
if(LotSize < MarketInfo(Symbol(),MODE_MINLOT))
  {
     LotSize = MarketInfo(Symbol(),MODE_MINLOT);
  }
else if(LotSize > MarketInfo(Symbol(),MODE_MAXLOT))
  {
     LotSize = MarketInfo(Symbol(),MODE_MAXLOT);
  }

if(MarketInfo(Symbol(),MODE_LOTSTEP) == 0.1)
  {
     LotSize = NormalizeDouble(LotSize,1);
  }
else LotSize = NormalizeDouble(LotSize,2);


// Buy Order
if(FastMA > SlowMA && BuyTicket == 0)
  {
     // Close Order
     OrderSelect(SellTicket,SELECT_BY_TICKET);

     if(OrderCloseTime() == 0 && SellTicket > 0)
       {
          double CloseLots = OrderLots();

          while(IsTradeContextBusy()) Sleep(10);

          RefreshRates();
          double ClosePrice = Ask;

          bool Closed = OrderClose(SellTicket,CloseLots,ClosePrice,UseSlippage,Red);

          // Error handling
          if(Closed == false)
            {
               ErrorCode = GetLastError();
               string ErrDesc = ErrorDescription(ErrorCode);
```

```
            string ErrAlert = StringConcatenate("Close Sell Order - Error ",
              ErrorCode,": ",ErrDesc);
            Alert(ErrAlert);

            string ErrLog = StringConcatenate("Ask: ",Ask," Lots: ",LotSize,
              " Ticket: ",SellTicket);
            Print(ErrLog);
         }

      }

   // Open buy order
   while(IsTradeContextBusy()) Sleep(10);
   RefreshRates();

   BuyTicket = OrderSend(Symbol(),OP_BUY,LotSize,Ask,UseSlippage,0,0,
      "Buy Order",MagicNumber,0,Green);

   // Error handling
   if(BuyTicket == -1)
      {
         ErrorCode = GetLastError();
         ErrDesc = ErrorDescription(ErrorCode);

         ErrAlert = StringConcatenate("Open Buy Order - Error ",ErrorCode,
            ": ",ErrDesc);
         Alert(ErrAlert);

         ErrLog = StringConcatenate("Ask: ",Ask," Lots: ",LotSize);
         Print(ErrLog);
      }

   // Order modification
   else
      {
         OrderSelect(BuyTicket,SELECT_BY_TICKET);
         double OpenPrice = OrderOpenPrice();

         // Calculate stop level
         double StopLevel = MarketInfo(Symbol(),MODE_STOPLEVEL) * Point;

         RefreshRates();
         double UpperStopLevel = Ask + StopLevel;
         double LowerStopLevel = Bid - StopLevel;

         double MinStop = 5 * UsePoint;

         // Calculate stop loss and take profit
         if(StopLoss > 0) double BuyStopLoss = OpenPrice - (StopLoss * UsePoint);

         if(TakeProfit > 0) double BuyTakeProfit = OpenPrice +
            (TakeProfit * UsePoint);
```

```
      // Verify stop loss and take profit
      if(BuyStopLoss > 0 && BuyStopLoss > LowerStopLevel)
        {
           BuyStopLoss = LowerStopLevel - MinStop;
        }

      if(BuyTakeProfit > 0 && BuyTakeProfit < UpperStopLevel)
        {
           BuyTakeProfit = UpperStopLevel + MinStop;
        }

      // Modify order
      if(IsTradeContextBusy()) Sleep(10);

      if(BuyStopLoss > 0 || BuyTakeProfit > 0)
        {
           bool TicketMod = OrderModify(BuyTicket,OpenPrice,BuyStopLoss,
             BuyTakeProfit,0);

           // Error handling
           if(TicketMod == false)
             {
                ErrorCode = GetLastError();
                ErrDesc = ErrorDescription(ErrorCode);

                ErrAlert = StringConcatenate("Modify Buy Order - Error ",ErrorCode,
                  ": ",ErrDesc);
                Alert(ErrAlert);

                ErrLog = StringConcatenate("Ask: ",Ask," Bid: ",Bid," Ticket: ",
                  BuyTicket," Stop: ",BuyStopLoss," Profit: ",BuyTakeProfit);
                Print(ErrLog);
             }
        }
    }

    SellTicket = 0;
  }


// Sell Order
if(FastMA < SlowMA && SellTicket == 0)
  {
    OrderSelect(BuyTicket,SELECT_BY_TICKET);

    if(OrderCloseTime() == 0 && BuyTicket > 0)
      {
         CloseLots = OrderLots();

         while(IsTradeContextBusy()) Sleep(10);

         RefreshRates();
```

163

```
            ClosePrice = Bid;

            Closed = OrderClose(BuyTicket,CloseLots,ClosePrice,UseSlippage,Red);

            // Error handling
            if(Closed == false)
              {
                ErrorCode = GetLastError();
                ErrDesc = ErrorDescription(ErrorCode);

                ErrAlert = StringConcatenate("Close Buy Order - Error ",ErrorCode,
                  ": ",ErrDesc);
                Alert(ErrAlert);

                ErrLog = StringConcatenate("Bid: ",Bid," Lots: ",LotSize," Ticket: ",
                  BuyTicket);
                Print(ErrLog);
              }
          }

    while(IsTradeContextBusy()) Sleep(10);
    RefreshRates();

    SellTicket = OrderSend(Symbol(),OP_SELL,LotSize,Bid,UseSlippage,0,0,
      "Sell Order", MagicNumber,0,Red);

    // Error handling
    if(SellTicket == -1)
      {
        ErrorCode = GetLastError();
        ErrDesc = ErrorDescription(ErrorCode);

        ErrAlert = StringConcatenate("Open Sell Order - Error ",ErrorCode,
          ": ",ErrDesc);
        Alert(ErrAlert);

        ErrLog = StringConcatenate("Bid: ",Bid," Lots: ",LotSize);
        Print(ErrLog);
      }

    else
      {
        OrderSelect(SellTicket,SELECT_BY_TICKET);
        OpenPrice = OrderOpenPrice();

        StopLevel = MarketInfo(Symbol(),MODE_STOPLEVEL) * Point;

        RefreshRates();
        UpperStopLevel = Ask + StopLevel;
        LowerStopLevel = Bid - StopLevel;

        MinStop = 5 * UsePoint;
        if(StopLoss > 0) double SellStopLoss = OpenPrice + (StopLoss * UsePoint);
```

```
        if(TakeProfit > 0) double SellTakeProfit = OpenPrice -
          (TakeProfit * UsePoint);

        if(SellStopLoss > 0 && SellStopLoss < UpperStopLevel)
          {
             SellStopLoss = UpperStopLevel + MinStop;
          }
        if(SellTakeProfit  > 0 && SellTakeProfit > LowerStopLevel)
          {
             SellTakeProfit = LowerStopLevel - MinStop;
          }

        if(IsTradeContextBusy()) Sleep(10);

        if(SellStopLoss > 0 || SellTakeProfit > 0)
          {
             TicketMod = OrderModify(SellTicket,OpenPrice,SellStopLoss,
               SellTakeProfit,0);

             // Error handling
             if(TicketMod == false)
               {
                  ErrorCode = GetLastError();
                  ErrDesc = ErrorDescription(ErrorCode);

                  ErrAlert = StringConcatenate("Modify Sell Order - Error ",
                    ErrorCode,": ",ErrDesc);
                  Alert(ErrAlert);

                  ErrLog = StringConcatenate("Ask: ",Ask," Bid: ",Bid," Ticket: ",
                    SellTicket," Stop: ",SellStopLoss," Profit: ",SellTakeProfit);
                  Print(ErrLog);
               }
          }
      }

     BuyTicket = 0;
   }
 return(0);
}


// Pip Point Function
double PipPoint(string Currency)
  {
    int CalcDigits = MarketInfo(Currency,MODE_DIGITS);
    if(CalcDigits == 2 || CalcDigits == 3) double CalcPoint = 0.01;
    else if(CalcDigits == 4 || CalcDigits == 5) CalcPoint = 0.0001;
    return(CalcPoint);
  }
```

```
// Get Slippage Function
int GetSlippage(string Currency, int SlippagePips)
  {
    int CalcDigits = MarketInfo(Currency,MODE_DIGITS);
    if(CalcDigits == 2 || CalcDigits == 4) double CalcSlippage = SlippagePips;
    else if(CalcDigits == 3 || CalcDigits == 5) CalcSlippage = SlippagePips * 10;
    return(CalcSlippage);
  }
```

Advanced Expert Advisor with Pending Orders

Here is the advanced expert advisor using pending stop orders:

```
#include <stdlib.mqh>

// External Variables
extern int PendingPips = 20;
extern double LotSize = 0.1;
extern double StopLoss = 50;
extern double TakeProfit = 100;
extern int Slippage = 5;
extern int MagicNumber = 123;
extern int FastMAPeriod = 10;
extern int SlowMAPeriod = 20;


// Global Variables
int BuyTicket;
int SellTicket;
double UsePoint;
int UseSlippage;
int ErrorCode;


// Init function
int init()
  {
    UsePoint = PipPoint(Symbol());
    UseSlippage = GetSlippage(Symbol(),Slippage);
  }


// Start Function
int start()
  {

    // Moving Average
    double FastMA = iMA(NULL,0,FastMAPeriod,0,0,0,0);
    double SlowMA = iMA(NULL,0,SlowMAPeriod,0,0,0,0);
```

```
// Buy Order
if(FastMA > SlowMA && BuyTicket == 0)
   {
     // Close order
     OrderSelect(SellTicket,SELECT_BY_TICKET);

     if(OrderCloseTime() == 0 && SellTicket > 0 && OrderType() == OP_SELL)
        {
          double CloseLots = OrderLots();

          while(IsTradeContextBusy()) Sleep(10);
          RefreshRates();
          double ClosePrice = Ask;

          bool Closed = OrderClose(SellTicket,CloseLots,ClosePrice,UseSlippage,Red);

          // Error handling
          if(Closed == false)
             {
               ErrorCode = GetLastError();
               string ErrDesc = ErrorDescription(ErrorCode);

               string ErrAlert = StringConcatenate("Close Sell Order - Error ",
                  ErrorCode,": ",ErrDesc);
               Alert(ErrAlert);

               string ErrLog = StringConcatenate("Ask: ",Ask," Lots: ",LotSize,
                  " Ticket: ",SellTicket);
               Print(ErrLog);
             }
        }

     // Delete order
     else if(OrderCloseTime() == 0 && SellTicket > 0 && OrderType() == OP_SELLSTOP)
        {
          bool Deleted = OrderDelete(SellTicket,Red);
          if(Deleted == true) SellTicket = 0;

          // Error handling
          if(Deleted == false)
             {
               ErrorCode = GetLastError();
               ErrDesc = ErrorDescription(ErrorCode);

               ErrAlert = StringConcatenate("Delete Sell Stop Order - Error ",
                  ErrorCode,": ",ErrDesc);
               Alert(ErrAlert);

               ErrLog = StringConcatenate("Ask: ",Ask," Ticket: ",SellTicket);
               Print(ErrLog);
             }
        }
```

167

```
   // Calculate stop level
   double StopLevel = MarketInfo(Symbol(),MODE_STOPLEVEL) * Point;
   RefreshRates();
   double UpperStopLevel = Ask + StopLevel;
   double MinStop = 5 * UsePoint;

   // Calculate pending price
   double PendingPrice = High[0] + (PendingPips * UsePoint);
   if(PendingPrice < UpperStopLevel) PendingPrice = UpperStopLevel + MinStop;

   // Calculate stop loss and take profit
   if(StopLoss > 0) double BuyStopLoss = PendingPrice - (StopLoss * UsePoint);
   if(TakeProfit > 0) double BuyTakeProfit = PendingPrice +
     (TakeProfit * UsePoint);

   // Verify stop loss and take profit
   UpperStopLevel = PendingPrice + StopLevel;
   double LowerStopLevel = PendingPrice - StopLevel;

   if(BuyStopLoss > 0 && BuyStopLoss > LowerStopLevel)
     {
        BuyStopLoss = LowerStopLevel - MinStop;
     }

   if(BuyTakeProfit  > 0 && BuyTakeProfit < UpperStopLevel)
     {
        BuyTakeProfit = UpperStopLevel + MinStop;
     }

   // Place pending order
   if(IsTradeContextBusy()) Sleep(10);

   BuyTicket = OrderSend(Symbol(),OP_BUYSTOP,LotSize,PendingPrice,UseSlippage,
     BuyStopLoss,BuyTakeProfit,"Buy Stop Order",MagicNumber,0,Green);

   // Error handling
   if(BuyTicket == -1)
     {
        ErrorCode = GetLastError();
        ErrDesc = ErrorDescription(ErrorCode);

        ErrAlert = StringConcatenate("Open Buy Stop Order - Error ",ErrorCode,
          ": ",ErrDesc);
        Alert(ErrAlert);

        ErrLog = StringConcatenate("Ask: ",Ask," Lots: ",LotSize," Price: ",
          PendingPrice," Stop: ",BuyStopLoss," Profit: ",BuyTakeProfit);
        Print(ErrLog);
     }

   SellTicket = 0;
}
```

```
// Sell Order
if(FastMA < SlowMA && SellTicket == 0)
   {
     OrderSelect(BuyTicket,SELECT_BY_TICKET);

     if(OrderCloseTime() == 0 && BuyTicket > 0 && OrderType() == OP_BUY)
        {
          CloseLots = OrderLots();

          while(IsTradeContextBusy()) Sleep(10);

          RefreshRates();
          ClosePrice = Bid;

          Closed = OrderClose(BuyTicket,CloseLots,ClosePrice,UseSlippage,Red);

          if(Closed == false)
             {
               ErrorCode = GetLastError();
               ErrDesc = ErrorDescription(ErrorCode);

               ErrAlert = StringConcatenate("Close Buy Order - Error ",ErrorCode,
                  ": ",ErrDesc);
               Alert(ErrAlert);

               ErrLog = StringConcatenate("Bid: ",Bid," Lots: ",LotSize," Ticket: ",
                  BuyTicket);
               Print(ErrLog);
             }
        }

     else if(OrderCloseTime() == 0 && BuyTicket > 0 && OrderType() == OP_BUYSTOP)
        {
          while(IsTradeContextBusy()) Sleep(10);
          Closed = OrderDelete(BuyTicket,Red);

          if(Deleted == false)
             {
               ErrorCode = GetLastError();
               ErrDesc = ErrorDescription(ErrorCode);

               ErrAlert = StringConcatenate("Delete Buy Stop Order - Error ",
                  ErrorCode,": ",ErrDesc);
               Alert(ErrAlert);

               ErrLog = StringConcatenate("Bid: ",Bid," Ticket: ",BuyTicket);
               Print(ErrLog);
             }
        }

     StopLevel = MarketInfo(Symbol(),MODE_STOPLEVEL) * Point;
     RefreshRates();
     LowerStopLevel = Bid - StopLevel;
```

```
         MinStop = 5 * UsePoint;

         PendingPrice = Low[0] - (PendingPips * UsePoint);
         if(PendingPrice > LowerStopLevel) PendingPrice = LowerStopLevel - MinStop;

         if(StopLoss > 0) double SellStopLoss = PendingPrice + (StopLoss * UsePoint);
         if(TakeProfit > 0) double SellTakeProfit = PendingPrice -
           (TakeProfit * UsePoint);

         UpperStopLevel = PendingPrice + StopLevel;
         LowerStopLevel = PendingPrice - StopLevel;

         if(SellStopLoss > 0 && SellStopLoss < UpperStopLevel)
           {
              SellStopLoss = UpperStopLevel + MinStop;
           }
         if(SellTakeProfit  > 0 && SellTakeProfit > LowerStopLevel)
           {
              SellTakeProfit = LowerStopLevel - MinStop;
           }

         if(IsTradeContextBusy()) Sleep(10);

         SellTicket = OrderSend(Symbol(),OP_SELLSTOP,LotSize,PendingPrice,UseSlippage,
           SellStopLoss,SellTakeProfit,"Sell Stop Order",MagicNumber,0,Red);

         if(SellTicket == -1)
           {
              ErrorCode = GetLastError();
              ErrDesc = ErrorDescription(ErrorCode);

              ErrAlert = StringConcatenate("Open Sell Stop Order - Error ",ErrorCode,
                ": ",ErrDesc);
              Alert(ErrAlert);

              ErrLog = StringConcatenate("Bid: ",Bid," Lots: ",LotSize," Price: ",
                PendingPrice," Stop: ",SellStopLoss," Profit: ",SellTakeProfit);
              Print(ErrLog);
           }

         BuyTicket = 0;
      }

   return(0);
}
```

```
// Pip Point Function
double PipPoint(string Currency)
  {
    int CalcDigits = MarketInfo(Currency,MODE_DIGITS);
    if(CalcDigits == 2 || CalcDigits == 3) double CalcPoint = 0.01;
    else if(CalcDigits == 4 || CalcDigits == 5) CalcPoint = 0.0001;
    return(CalcPoint);
  }


// Get Slippage Function
int GetSlippage(string Currency, int SlippagePips)
  {
    int CalcDigits = MarketInfo(Currency,MODE_DIGITS);
    if(CalcDigits == 2 || CalcDigits == 4) double CalcSlippage = SlippagePips;
    else if(CalcDigits == 3 || CalcDigits == 5) CalcSlippage = SlippagePips * 10;
    return(CalcSlippage);
  }
```

Appendix C

Expert Advisor with Functions

This is the expert advisor using the functions introduced in chapter 4. We've added the "close all orders" functions and trailing stop function from chapter 5, and the "execute once per bar" features from chapter 7.

The functions are defined in **IncludeExample.mqh**, the contents of which are listed in Appendix D.

```
// Preprocessor
#property copyright "Andrew Young"
#include <IncludeExample.mqh>


// External variables
extern bool DynamicLotSize = true;
extern double EquityPercent = 2;
extern double FixedLotSize = 0.1;

extern double StopLoss = 50;
extern double TakeProfit = 100;

extern int TrailingStop = 50;
extern int MinimumProfit = 50;

extern int Slippage = 5;
extern int MagicNumber = 123;

extern int FastMAPeriod = 10;
extern int SlowMAPeriod = 20;

extern bool CheckOncePerBar = true;


// Global variables
int BuyTicket;
int SellTicket;

double UsePoint;
int UseSlippage;

datetime CurrentTimeStamp;
```

```
// Init function
int init()
  {
    UsePoint = PipPoint(Symbol());
    UseSlippage = GetSlippage(Symbol(),Slippage);
  }


// Start function
int start()
  {

    // Execute on bar open
    if(CheckOncePerBar == true)
      {
        int BarShift = 1;
        if(CurrentTimeStamp != Time[0])
          {
            CurrentTimeStamp = Time[0];
            bool NewBar = true;
          }
        else NewBar = false;
      }
    else
      {
        NewBar = true;
        BarShift = 0;
      }


    // Moving averages
    double FastMA = iMA(NULL,0,FastMAPeriod,0,0,0,BarShift);
    double SlowMA = iMA(NULL,0,SlowMAPeriod,0,0,0,BarShift);

    double LastFastMA = iMA(NULL,0,FastMAPeriod,0,0,0,BarShift+1);
    double LastSlowMA = iMA(NULL,0,SlowMAPeriod,0,0,0,BarShift+1);


    // Calculate lot size
    double LotSize = CalcLotSize(DynamicLotSize,EquityPercent,StopLoss,FixedLotSize);
    LotSize = VerifyLotSize(LotSize);


    // Begin trade block
    if(NewBar == true)
      {

        // Buy order
        if(FastMA > SlowMA && LastFastMA <= LastSlowMA &&
          BuyMarketCount(Symbol(),MagicNumber) == 0)
          {
```

173

```
   // Close sell orders
   if(SellMarketCount(Symbol(),MagicNumber) > 0)
     {
        CloseAllSellOrders(Symbol(),MagicNumber,Slippage);
     }

   // Open buy order
   BuyTicket = OpenBuyOrder(Symbol(),LotSize,UseSlippage,MagicNumber);

   // Order modification
   if(BuyTicket > 0 && (StopLoss > 0 || TakeProfit > 0))
     {
        OrderSelect(BuyTicket,SELECT_BY_TICKET);
        double OpenPrice = OrderOpenPrice();

        // Calculate and verify stop loss and take profit
        double BuyStopLoss = CalcBuyStopLoss(Symbol(),StopLoss,OpenPrice);
        if(BuyStopLoss > 0) BuyStopLoss = AdjustBelowStopLevel(Symbol(),
          BuyStopLoss,5);

        double BuyTakeProfit = CalcBuyTakeProfit(Symbol(),TakeProfit,
          OpenPrice);
        if(BuyTakeProfit > 0) BuyTakeProfit = AdjustAboveStopLevel(Symbol(),
          BuyTakeProfit,5);

        // Add stop loss and take profit
        AddStopProfit(BuyTicket,BuyStopLoss,BuyTakeProfit);
     }
 }


// Sell Order
if(FastMA < SlowMA && LastFastMA >= LastSlowMA
  && SellMarketCount(Symbol(),MagicNumber) == 0)
  {
    if(BuyMarketCount(Symbol(),MagicNumber) > 0)
      {
         CloseAllBuyOrders(Symbol(),MagicNumber,Slippage);
      }

    SellTicket = OpenSellOrder(Symbol(),LotSize,UseSlippage,MagicNumber);

    if(SellTicket > 0 && (StopLoss > 0 || TakeProfit > 0))
      {
         OrderSelect(SellTicket,SELECT_BY_TICKET);
         OpenPrice = OrderOpenPrice();

         double SellStopLoss = CalcSellStopLoss(Symbol(),StopLoss,OpenPrice);
         if(SellStopLoss > 0) SellStopLoss = AdjustAboveStopLevel(Symbol(),
           SellStopLoss,5);

         double SellTakeProfit = CalcSellTakeProfit(Symbol(),TakeProfit,
           OpenPrice);
```

174

```
                if(SellTakeProfit > 0) SellTakeProfit = AdjustBelowStopLevel(Symbol(),
                  SellTakeProfit,5);

                AddStopProfit(SellTicket,SellStopLoss,SellTakeProfit);
              }
          }

      }  // End trade block


      // Adjust trailing stops
      if(BuyMarketCount(Symbol(),MagicNumber) > 0 && TrailingStop > 0)
        {
          BuyTrailingStop(Symbol(),TrailingStop,MinimumProfit,MagicNumber);
        }

      if(SellMarketCount(Symbol(),MagicNumber) > 0 && TrailingStop > 0)
        {
          SellTrailingStop(Symbol(),TrailingStop,MinimumProfit,MagicNumber);
        }


      return(0);
    }
```

Expert Advisor with Functions – Pending Orders

This is the expert advisor with functions, using pending stop orders:

```
// Preprocessor
#property copyright "Andrew Young"
#include <IncludeExample.mqh>


// External variables
extern bool DynamicLotSize = true;
extern double EquityPercent = 2;
extern double FixedLotSize = 0.1;

extern double StopLoss = 50;
extern double TakeProfit = 100;

extern int TrailingStop = 50;
extern int MinimumProfit = 50;

extern int PendingPips = 1;

extern int Slippage = 5;
extern int MagicNumber = 123;
```

```
extern int FastMAPeriod = 10;
extern int SlowMAPeriod = 20;

extern bool CheckOncePerBar = true;


// Global Variables
int BuyTicket;
int SellTicket;

double UsePoint;
int UseSlippage;

datetime CurrentTimeStamp;


// Init function
int init()
  {
    UsePoint = PipPoint(Symbol());
    UseSlippage = GetSlippage(Symbol(),Slippage);

    CurrentTimeStamp = Time[0];
  }


// Start Function
int start()
  {
    // Execute on bar open
    if(CheckOncePerBar == true)
      {
        int BarShift = 1;
        if(CurrentTimeStamp != Time[0])
          {
            CurrentTimeStamp = Time[0];
            bool NewBar = true;
          }
        else NewBar = false;
      }
    else
      {
        NewBar = true;
        BarShift = 0;
      }


    // Moving averages
    double FastMA = iMA(NULL,0,FastMAPeriod,0,0,0,BarShift);
    double SlowMA = iMA(NULL,0,SlowMAPeriod,0,0,0,BarShift);
```

```
// Calculate lot size
double LotSize = CalcLotSize(DynamicLotSize,EquityPercent,StopLoss,FixedLotSize);
LotSize = VerifyLotSize(LotSize);


// Begin trade block
if(NewBar == true)
  {

    // Buy order
    if(FastMA > SlowMA && BuyTicket == 0 && BuyMarketCount(Symbol(),MagicNumber)
      == 0 && BuyStopCount(Symbol(),MagicNumber) == 0)
      {
        // Close sell order
        if(SellMarketCount(Symbol(),MagicNumber) > 0)
          {
            CloseAllSellOrders(Symbol(),MagicNumber,Slippage);
          }

        // Delete sell stop order
        if(SellStopCount(Symbol(),MagicNumber) > 0)
          {
            CloseAllSellStopOrders(Symbol(),MagicNumber);
          }

        SellTicket = 0;

        double PendingPrice = High[BarShift] + (PendingPips * UsePoint);
        PendingPrice = AdjustAboveStopLevel(Symbol(),PendingPrice,5);

        double BuyStopLoss = CalcBuyStopLoss(Symbol(),StopLoss,PendingPrice);
        if(BuyStopLoss > 0) BuyStopLoss = AdjustBelowStopLevel(Symbol(),BuyStopLoss,
          5,PendingPrice);

        double BuyTakeProfit = CalcBuyTakeProfit(Symbol(),TakeProfit,PendingPrice);
        if(BuyTakeProfit > 0) BuyTakeProfit = AdjustAboveStopLevel(Symbol(),
          BuyTakeProfit,5,PendingPrice);

        BuyTicket = OpenBuyLimitOrder(Symbol(),LotSize,PendingPrice,BuyStopLoss,
          BuyTakeProfit,UseSlippage,MagicNumber);
      }


    // Sell Order
    if(FastMA < SlowMA && SellTicket == 0
      && SellMarketCount(Symbol(),MagicNumber) == 0
      && SellStopCount(Symbol(),MagicNumber) == 0)
      {
        if(BuyMarketCount(Symbol(),MagicNumber) > 0)
          {
            CloseAllBuyOrders(Symbol(),MagicNumber,Slippage);
          }
```

177

```
            if(BuyStopCount(Symbol(),MagicNumber) > 0)
              {
                CloseAllBuyStopOrders(Symbol(),MagicNumber);
              }

            BuyTicket = 0;

            PendingPrice = Low[BarShift] - (PendingPips * UsePoint);
            PendingPrice = AdjustBelowStopLevel(Symbol(),PendingPrice,5);

            double SellStopLoss = CalcSellStopLoss(Symbol(),StopLoss,PendingPrice);
            if(SellStopLoss > 0) SellStopLoss = AdjustAboveStopLevel(Symbol(),
              SellStopLoss,5,PendingPrice);

            double SellTakeProfit = CalcSellTakeProfit(Symbol(),TakeProfit,
              PendingPrice);
            if(SellTakeProfit > 0) AdjustBelowStopLevel(Symbol(),
              SellTakeProfit,5,PendingPrice);

            SellTicket = OpenSellLimitOrder(Symbol(),LotSize,PendingPrice,SellStopLoss,
              SellTakeProfit,UseSlippage,MagicNumber);
          }

      }  // End trade block


  // Adjust trailing stops
  if(BuyMarketCount(Symbol(),MagicNumber) > 0 && TrailingStop > 0)
    {
      BuyTrailingStop(Symbol(),TrailingStop,MinimumProfit,MagicNumber);
    }

  if(SellMarketCount(Symbol(),MagicNumber) > 0 && TrailingStop > 0)
    {
      SellTrailingStop(Symbol(),TrailingStop,MinimumProfit,MagicNumber);
    }


  return(0);
}
```

Appendix D

Include File

This is the include file with the functions used in the expert advisor in Appendix C.

```
#property copyright "Andrew Young"
#include <stdlib.mqh>


double CalcLotSize(bool argDynamicLotSize, double argEquityPercent,double argStopLoss,
   double argFixedLotSize)
   {
      if(argDynamicLotSize == true && argStopLoss > 0)
         {
            double RiskAmount = AccountEquity() * (argEquityPercent / 100);
            double TickValue = MarketInfo(Symbol(),MODE_TICKVALUE);
            if(Point == 0.001 || Point == 0.00001) TickValue *= 10;
            double LotSize = (RiskAmount / argStopLoss) / TickValue;
         }
      else LotSize = argFixedLotSize;

      return(LotSize);
   }


double VerifyLotSize(double argLotSize)
   {
      if(argLotSize < MarketInfo(Symbol(),MODE_MINLOT))
         {
            argLotSize = MarketInfo(Symbol(),MODE_MINLOT);
         }
      else if(argLotSize > MarketInfo(Symbol(),MODE_MAXLOT))
         {
            argLotSize = MarketInfo(Symbol(),MODE_MAXLOT);
         }

      if(MarketInfo(Symbol(),MODE_LOTSTEP) == 0.1)
         {
            argLotSize = NormalizeDouble(argLotSize,1);
         }
      else argLotSize = NormalizeDouble(argLotSize,2);

      return(argLotSize);
   }
```

```
int OpenBuyOrder(string argSymbol, double argLotSize, double argSlippage,
    double argMagicNumber, string argComment = "Buy Order")
  {
    while(IsTradeContextBusy()) Sleep(10);

    // Place Buy Order
    int Ticket = OrderSend(argSymbol,OP_BUY,argLotSize,MarketInfo(argSymbol,MODE_ASK),
      argSlippage,0,0,argComment,argMagicNumber,0,Green);

    // Error Handling
    if(Ticket == -1)
      {
        int ErrorCode = GetLastError();
        string ErrDesc = ErrorDescription(ErrorCode);

        string ErrAlert = StringConcatenate("Open Buy Order - Error ",ErrorCode,": ",
          ErrDesc);
        Alert(ErrAlert);

        string ErrLog = StringConcatenate("Bid: ",MarketInfo(argSymbol,MODE_BID),
          " Ask: ",MarketInfo(argSymbol,MODE_ASK)," Lots: ",argLotSize);
        Print(ErrLog);
      }
    return(Ticket);
  }


int OpenSellOrder(string argSymbol, double argLotSize, double argSlippage,
    double argMagicNumber, string argComment = "Sell Order")
  {
    while(IsTradeContextBusy()) Sleep(10);

    // Place Sell Order
    int Ticket = OrderSend(argSymbol,OP_SELL,argLotSize,MarketInfo(argSymbol,MODE_BID),
      argSlippage,0,0,argComment,argMagicNumber,0,Red);

    // Error Handling
    if(Ticket == -1)
      {
        int ErrorCode = GetLastError();
        string ErrDesc = ErrorDescription(ErrorCode);

        string ErrAlert = StringConcatenate("Open Sell Order - Error ",ErrorCode,
          ": ",ErrDesc);
        Alert(ErrAlert);

        string ErrLog = StringConcatenate("Bid: ",MarketInfo(argSymbol,MODE_BID),
          " Ask: ",MarketInfo(argSymbol,MODE_ASK)," Lots: ",argLotSize);
        Print(ErrLog);
      }
    return(Ticket);
  }
```

```
int OpenBuyStopOrder(string argSymbol, double argLotSize, double argPendingPrice,
   double argStopLoss, double argTakeProfit, double argSlippage, double argMagicNumber,
   datetime argExpiration = 0, string argComment = "Buy Stop Order")
   {
      while(IsTradeContextBusy()) Sleep(10);

      // Place Buy Stop Order
      int Ticket = OrderSend(argSymbol,OP_BUYSTOP,argLotSize,argPendingPrice,argSlippage,
         argStopLoss,argTakeProfit,argComment,argMagicNumber,argExpiration,Green);

      // Error Handling
      if(Ticket == -1)
         {
            int ErrorCode = GetLastError();
            string ErrDesc = ErrorDescription(ErrorCode);

            string ErrAlert = StringConcatenate("Open Buy Stop Order - Error ",ErrorCode,
               ": ",ErrDesc);
            Alert(ErrAlert);

            string ErrLog = StringConcatenate("Ask: ",MarketInfo(argSymbol,MODE_ASK),
               " Lots: ",argLotSize," Price: ",argPendingPrice," Stop: ",argStopLoss,
               " Profit: ",argTakeProfit," Expiration: ",TimeToStr(argExpiration));
            Print(ErrLog);
         }

      return(Ticket);
   }


int OpenSellStopOrder(string argSymbol, double argLotSize, double argPendingPrice,
   double argStopLoss, double argTakeProfit, double argSlippage, double argMagicNumber,
   datetime argExpiration = 0, string argComment = "Sell Stop Order")
   {
      while(IsTradeContextBusy()) Sleep(10);

      // Place Sell Stop Order
      int Ticket = OrderSend(argSymbol,OP_SELLSTOP,argLotSize,argPendingPrice,argSlippage,
         argStopLoss,argTakeProfit,argComment,argMagicNumber,argExpiration,Red);

      // Error Handling
      if(Ticket == -1)
         {
            int ErrorCode = GetLastError();
            string ErrDesc = ErrorDescription(ErrorCode);

            string ErrAlert = StringConcatenate("Open Sell Stop Order - Error ",ErrorCode,
               ": ",ErrDesc);
            Alert(ErrAlert);

            string ErrLog = StringConcatenate("Bid: ",MarketInfo(argSymbol,MODE_BID),
               " Lots: ",argLotSize," Price: ",argPendingPrice," Stop: ",argStopLoss,
               " Profit: ",argTakeProfit," Expiration: ",TimeToStr(argExpiration));
```

```
            Print(ErrLog);
         }

      return(Ticket);
   }


int OpenBuyLimitOrder(string argSymbol, double argLotSize, double argPendingPrice,
   double argStopLoss, double argTakeProfit, double argSlippage, double argMagicNumber,
   datetime argExpiration, string argComment = "Buy Limit Order")
   {
      while(IsTradeContextBusy()) Sleep(10);

      // Place Buy Limit Order
      int Ticket = OrderSend(argSymbol,OP_BUYLIMIT,argLotSize,argPendingPrice,argSlippage,
         argStopLoss,argTakeProfit,argComment,argMagicNumber,argExpiration,Green);

      // Error Handling
      if(Ticket == -1)
        {
           int ErrorCode = GetLastError();
           string ErrDesc = ErrorDescription(ErrorCode);

           string ErrAlert = StringConcatenate("Open Buy Limit Order - Error ",ErrorCode,
              ": ",ErrDesc);
           Alert(ErrAlert);

           string ErrLog = StringConcatenate("Bid: ",MarketInfo(argSymbol,MODE_BID),
              " Lots: ",argLotSize," Price: ",argPendingPrice," Stop: ",argStopLoss,
              " Profit: ",argTakeProfit," Expiration: ",TimeToStr(argExpiration));
           Print(ErrLog);
        }

      return(Ticket);
   }


int OpenSellLimitOrder(string argSymbol, double argLotSize, double argPendingPrice,
   double argStopLoss, double argTakeProfit, double argSlippage, double argMagicNumber,
   datetime argExpiration, string argComment = "Sell Limit Order")
   {
      while(IsTradeContextBusy()) Sleep(10);

      // Place Sell Limit Order
      int Ticket = OrderSend(argSymbol,OP_SELLLIMIT,argLotSize,argPendingPrice,argSlippage,
         argStopLoss,argTakeProfit,argComment,argMagicNumber,argExpiration,Red);

      // Error Handling
      if(Ticket == -1)
        {
           int ErrorCode = GetLastError();
           string ErrDesc = ErrorDescription(ErrorCode);
```

```
            string ErrAlert = StringConcatenate("Open Sell Stop Order - Error ",ErrorCode,
              ": ",ErrDesc);
            Alert(ErrAlert);

            string ErrLog = StringConcatenate("Ask: ",MarketInfo(argSymbol,MODE_ASK),
              " Lots: ",argLotSize," Price: ",argPendingPrice," Stop: ",argStopLoss,
              " Profit: ",argTakeProfit," Expiration: ",TimeToStr(argExpiration));
            Print(ErrLog);
          }
       return(Ticket);
    }


double PipPoint(string Currency)
  {
    int CalcDigits = MarketInfo(Currency,MODE_DIGITS);
    if(CalcDigits == 2 || CalcDigits == 3) double CalcPoint = 0.01;
    else if(CalcDigits == 4 || CalcDigits == 5) CalcPoint = 0.0001;
    return(CalcPoint);
  }


int GetSlippage(string Currency, int SlippagePips)
  {
    int CalcDigits = MarketInfo(Currency,MODE_DIGITS);
    if(CalcDigits == 2 || CalcDigits == 4) double CalcSlippage = SlippagePips;
    else if(CalcDigits == 3 || CalcDigits == 5) CalcSlippage = SlippagePips * 10;
    return(CalcSlippage);
  }


bool CloseBuyOrder(string argSymbol, int argCloseTicket, double argSlippage)
  {
    OrderSelect(argCloseTicket,SELECT_BY_TICKET);

    if(OrderCloseTime() == 0)
      {
        double CloseLots = OrderLots();

        while(IsTradeContextBusy()) Sleep(10);

        double ClosePrice = MarketInfo(argSymbol,MODE_BID);
        bool Closed = OrderClose(argCloseTicket,CloseLots,ClosePrice,argSlippage,Green);

        if(Closed == false)
          {
            int ErrorCode = GetLastError();
            string ErrDesc = ErrorDescription(ErrorCode);

            string ErrAlert = StringConcatenate("Close Buy Order - Error: ",ErrorCode,
              ": ",ErrDesc);
            Alert(ErrAlert);
```

184

```
                   string ErrLog = StringConcatenate("Ticket: ",argCloseTicket," Bid: ",
                     MarketInfo(argSymbol,MODE_BID));
                   Print(ErrLog);
                 }
           }

        return(Closed);
     }


bool CloseSellOrder(string argSymbol, int argCloseTicket, double argSlippage)
   {
      OrderSelect(argCloseTicket,SELECT_BY_TICKET);

      if(OrderCloseTime() == 0)
        {
           double CloseLots = OrderLots();

           while(IsTradeContextBusy()) Sleep(10);

           double ClosePrice = MarketInfo(argSymbol,MODE_ASK);
           bool Closed = OrderClose(argCloseTicket,CloseLots,ClosePrice,argSlippage,Red);

           if(Closed == false)
             {
                int ErrorCode = GetLastError();
                string ErrDesc = ErrorDescription(ErrorCode);

                string ErrAlert = StringConcatenate("Close Sell Order - Error: ",ErrorCode,
                   ": ",ErrDesc);
                Alert(ErrAlert);

                string ErrLog = StringConcatenate("Ticket: ",argCloseTicket,
                   " Ask: ",MarketInfo(argSymbol,MODE_ASK));
                Print(ErrLog);
             }
        }
      return(Closed);
   }


bool ClosePendingOrder(string argSymbol, int argCloseTicket)
   {
      OrderSelect(argCloseTicket,SELECT_BY_TICKET);

      if(OrderCloseTime() == 0)
        {
           while(IsTradeContextBusy()) Sleep(10);
           bool Deleted = OrderDelete(argCloseTicket,Red);

           if(Deleted == false)
             {
                int ErrorCode = GetLastError();
```

```
                 string ErrDesc = ErrorDescription(ErrorCode);

                 string ErrAlert = StringConcatenate("Close Pending Order - Error: ",
                   ErrorCode,": ",ErrDesc);
                 Alert(ErrAlert);

                 string ErrLog = StringConcatenate("Ticket: ",argCloseTicket," Bid: ",
                   MarketInfo(argSymbol,MODE_BID)," Ask: ",MarketInfo(argSymbol,MODE_ASK));
                 Print(ErrLog);
              }
           }
        return(Deleted);
     }


double CalcBuyStopLoss(string argSymbol, int argStopLoss, double argOpenPrice)
   {
      if(argStopLoss == 0) return(0);

      double BuyStopLoss = argOpenPrice - (argStopLoss * PipPoint(argSymbol));
      return(BuyStopLoss);
   }


double CalcSellStopLoss(string argSymbol, int argStopLoss, double argOpenPrice)
   {
      if(argStopLoss == 0) return(0);

      double SellStopLoss = argOpenPrice + (argStopLoss * PipPoint(argSymbol));
      return(SellStopLoss);
   }


double CalcBuyTakeProfit(string argSymbol, int argTakeProfit, double argOpenPrice)
   {
      if(argTakeProfit == 0) return(0);

      double BuyTakeProfit = argOpenPrice + (argTakeProfit * PipPoint(argSymbol));
      return(BuyTakeProfit);
   }


double CalcSellTakeProfit(string argSymbol, int argTakeProfit, double argOpenPrice)
   {
      if(argTakeProfit == 0) return(0);

      double SellTakeProfit = argOpenPrice - (argTakeProfit * PipPoint(argSymbol));
      return(SellTakeProfit);
   }
```

```
bool VerifyUpperStopLevel(string argSymbol, double argVerifyPrice,
   double argOpenPrice = 0)
   {
      double StopLevel = MarketInfo(argSymbol,MODE_STOPLEVEL) * Point;

      if(argOpenPrice == 0) double OpenPrice = MarketInfo(argSymbol,MODE_ASK);
      else OpenPrice = argOpenPrice;

      double UpperStopLevel = OpenPrice + StopLevel;

      if(argVerifyPrice > UpperStopLevel) bool StopVerify = true;
      else StopVerify = false;

      return(StopVerify);
   }


bool VerifyLowerStopLevel(string argSymbol, double argVerifyPrice,
   double argOpenPrice = 0)
   {
      double StopLevel = MarketInfo(argSymbol,MODE_STOPLEVEL) * Point;

      if(argOpenPrice == 0) double OpenPrice = MarketInfo(argSymbol,MODE_BID);
      else OpenPrice = argOpenPrice;

      double LowerStopLevel = OpenPrice - StopLevel;

      if(argVerifyPrice < LowerStopLevel) bool StopVerify = true;
      else StopVerify = false;

      return(StopVerify);
   }


double AdjustAboveStopLevel(string argSymbol, double argAdjustPrice, int argAddPips = 0,
   double argOpenPrice = 0)
   {
      double StopLevel = MarketInfo(argSymbol,MODE_STOPLEVEL) * Point;

      if(argOpenPrice == 0) double OpenPrice = MarketInfo(argSymbol,MODE_ASK);
      else OpenPrice = argOpenPrice;

      double UpperStopLevel = OpenPrice + StopLevel;

      if(argAdjustPrice <= UpperStopLevel) double AdjustedPrice = UpperStopLevel +
         (argAddPips * PipPoint(argSymbol));
      else AdjustedPrice = argAdjustPrice;

      return(AdjustedPrice);
   }
```

```
double AdjustBelowStopLevel(string argSymbol, double argAdjustPrice, int argAddPips = 0,
  double argOpenPrice = 0)
  {
     double StopLevel = MarketInfo(argSymbol,MODE_STOPLEVEL) * Point;

     if(argOpenPrice == 0) double OpenPrice = MarketInfo(argSymbol,MODE_BID);
     else OpenPrice = argOpenPrice;

     double LowerStopLevel = OpenPrice - StopLevel;

     if(argAdjustPrice >= LowerStopLevel) double AdjustedPrice = LowerStopLevel -
       (argAddPips * PipPoint(argSymbol));
     else AdjustedPrice = argAdjustPrice;

     return(AdjustedPrice);
  }


bool AddStopProfit(int argTicket, double argStopLoss, double argTakeProfit)
  {
     OrderSelect(argTicket,SELECT_BY_TICKET);
     double OpenPrice = OrderOpenPrice();

     while(IsTradeContextBusy()) Sleep(10);

     // Modify Order
     bool TicketMod = OrderModify(argTicket,OrderOpenPrice(),argStopLoss,argTakeProfit,0);

     // Error Handling
     if(TicketMod == false)
       {
          int ErrorCode = GetLastError();
          string ErrDesc = ErrorDescription(ErrorCode);

          string ErrAlert = StringConcatenate("Add Stop/Profit - Error ",ErrorCode,
            ": ",ErrDesc);
          Alert(ErrAlert);

          string ErrLog = StringConcatenate("Bid: ",MarketInfo(OrderSymbol(),MODE_BID),
            " Ask: ",MarketInfo(OrderSymbol(),MODE_ASK)," Ticket: ",argTicket," Stop: ",
            argStopLoss," Profit: ",argTakeProfit);
          Print(ErrLog);
       }
     return(TicketMod);
  }
```

```
int TotalOrderCount(string argSymbol, int argMagicNumber)
  {
    int OrderCount;
    for(int Counter = 0; Counter <= OrdersTotal()-1; Counter++)
      {
        OrderSelect(Counter,SELECT_BY_POS);
        if(OrderMagicNumber() == argMagicNumber && OrderSymbol() == argSymbol)
          {
            OrderCount++;
          }
      }
    return(OrderCount);
  }


int BuyMarketCount(string argSymbol, int argMagicNumber)
  {
    int OrderCount;
    for(int Counter = 0; Counter <= OrdersTotal()-1; Counter++)
      {
        OrderSelect(Counter,SELECT_BY_POS);
        if(OrderMagicNumber() == argMagicNumber && OrderSymbol() == argSymbol
          && OrderType() == OP_BUY)
          {
            OrderCount++;
          }
      }
    return(OrderCount);
  }


int SellMarketCount(string argSymbol, int argMagicNumber)
  {
    int OrderCount;
    for(int Counter = 0; Counter <= OrdersTotal()-1; Counter++)
      {
        OrderSelect(Counter,SELECT_BY_POS);
        if(OrderMagicNumber() == argMagicNumber && OrderSymbol() == argSymbol
          && OrderType() == OP_SELL)
          {
            OrderCount++;
          }
      }
    return(OrderCount);
  }
```

```
int BuyStopCount(string argSymbol, int argMagicNumber)
  {
    int OrderCount;
    for(int Counter = 0; Counter <= OrdersTotal()-1; Counter++)
      {
        OrderSelect(Counter,SELECT_BY_POS);
        if(OrderMagicNumber() == argMagicNumber && OrderSymbol() == argSymbol
          && OrderType() == OP_BUYSTOP)
          {
            OrderCount++;
          }
      }
    return(OrderCount);
  }


int SellStopCount(string argSymbol, int argMagicNumber)
  {
    int OrderCount;
    for(int Counter = 0; Counter <= OrdersTotal()-1; Counter++)
      {
        OrderSelect(Counter,SELECT_BY_POS);
        if(OrderMagicNumber() == argMagicNumber && OrderSymbol() == argSymbol
          && OrderType() == OP_SELLSTOP)
          {
            OrderCount++;
          }
      }
    return(OrderCount);
  }


int BuyLimitCount(string argSymbol, int argMagicNumber)
  {
    int OrderCount;
    for(int Counter = 0; Counter <= OrdersTotal()-1; Counter++)
      {
        OrderSelect(Counter,SELECT_BY_POS);
        if(OrderMagicNumber() == argMagicNumber && OrderSymbol() == argSymbol
          && OrderType() == OP_BUYLIMIT)
          {
            OrderCount++;
          }
      }
    return(OrderCount);
  }
```

```
int SellLimitCount(string argSymbol, int argMagicNumber)
  {
    int OrderCount;
    for(int Counter = 0; Counter <= OrdersTotal()-1; Counter++)
      {
        OrderSelect(Counter,SELECT_BY_POS);
        if(OrderMagicNumber() == argMagicNumber && OrderSymbol() == argSymbol
          && OrderType() == OP_SELLLIMIT)
          {
            OrderCount++;
          }
      }
    return(OrderCount);
  }


void CloseAllBuyOrders(string argSymbol, int argMagicNumber, int argSlippage)
  {
    for(int Counter = 0; Counter <= OrdersTotal()-1; Counter++)
      {
        OrderSelect(Counter,SELECT_BY_POS);

        if(OrderMagicNumber() == argMagicNumber && OrderSymbol() == argSymbol
          && OrderType() == OP_BUY)
          {
            // Close Order
            int CloseTicket = OrderTicket();
            double CloseLots = OrderLots();

            while(IsTradeContextBusy()) Sleep(10);
            double ClosePrice = MarketInfo(argSymbol,MODE_BID);

            bool Closed = OrderClose(CloseTicket,CloseLots,ClosePrice,argSlippage,Red);

            // Error Handling
            if(Closed == false)
              {
                int ErrorCode = GetLastError();
                string ErrDesc = ErrorDescription(ErrorCode);

                string ErrAlert = StringConcatenate("Close All Buy Orders - Error ",
                  ErrorCode,": ",ErrDesc);
                Alert(ErrAlert);

                string ErrLog = StringConcatenate("Bid: ",
                  MarketInfo(argSymbol,MODE_BID)," Ticket: ",CloseTicket," Price: ",
                  ClosePrice);
                Print(ErrLog);
              }
            else Counter--;
          }
      }
  }
```

```
void CloseAllSellOrders(string argSymbol, int argMagicNumber, int argSlippage)
  {
    for(int Counter = 0; Counter <= OrdersTotal()-1; Counter++)
      {
        OrderSelect(Counter,SELECT_BY_POS);

        if(OrderMagicNumber() == argMagicNumber && OrderSymbol() == argSymbol
          && OrderType() == OP_SELL)
          {
            // Close Order
            int CloseTicket = OrderTicket();
            double CloseLots = OrderLots();

            while(IsTradeContextBusy()) Sleep(10);

            double ClosePrice = MarketInfo(argSymbol,MODE_ASK);

            bool Closed = OrderClose(CloseTicket,CloseLots,ClosePrice,argSlippage,Red);

            // Error Handling
            if(Closed == false)
              {
                int ErrorCode = GetLastError();
                string ErrDesc = ErrorDescription(ErrorCode);

                string ErrAlert = StringConcatenate("Close All Sell Orders - Error ",
                  ErrorCode,": ",ErrDesc);
                Alert(ErrAlert);

                string ErrLog = StringConcatenate("Ask: ",
                  MarketInfo(argSymbol,MODE_ASK)," Ticket: ",CloseTicket," Price: ",
                  ClosePrice);
                Print(ErrLog);
              }
            else Counter--;
          }
      }
  }


void CloseAllBuyStopOrders(string argSymbol, int argMagicNumber)
  {
    for(int Counter = 0; Counter <= OrdersTotal()-1; Counter++)
      {
        OrderSelect(Counter,SELECT_BY_POS);

        if(OrderMagicNumber() == argMagicNumber && OrderSymbol() == argSymbol
          && OrderType() == OP_BUYSTOP)
          {
            // Delete Order
            int CloseTicket = OrderTicket();
```

```
            while(IsTradeContextBusy()) Sleep(10);
            bool Closed = OrderDelete(CloseTicket,Red);

            // Error Handling
            if(Closed == false)
              {
                 int ErrorCode = GetLastError();
                 string ErrDesc = ErrorDescription(ErrorCode);

                 string ErrAlert = StringConcatenate("Close All Buy Stop Orders - ",
                   "Error",ErrorCode,": ",ErrDesc);
                 Alert(ErrAlert);


                 string ErrLog = StringConcatenate("Bid: ",
                   MarketInfo(argSymbol,MODE_BID)," Ask: ",
                   MarketInfo(argSymbol,MODE_ASK)," Ticket: ",CloseTicket);
                 Print(ErrLog);
              }
            else Counter--;
          }
      }
  }


void CloseAllSellStopOrders(string argSymbol, int argMagicNumber)
  {
    for(int Counter = 0; Counter <= OrdersTotal()-1; Counter++)
      {
        OrderSelect(Counter,SELECT_BY_POS);

        if(OrderMagicNumber() == argMagicNumber && OrderSymbol() == argSymbol
          && OrderType() == OP_SELLSTOP)
          {
            // Delete Order
            int CloseTicket = OrderTicket();

            while(IsTradeContextBusy()) Sleep(10);

            bool Closed = OrderDelete(CloseTicket,Red);

            // Error Handling
            if(Closed == false)
              {
                 int ErrorCode = GetLastError();
                 string ErrDesc = ErrorDescription(ErrorCode);

                 string ErrAlert = StringConcatenate("Close All Sell Stop Orders - ",
                   "Error ",ErrorCode,": ",ErrDesc);
                 Alert(ErrAlert);
```

```
            string ErrLog = StringConcatenate("Bid: ",
              MarketInfo(argSymbol,MODE_BID)," Ask: ",
              MarketInfo(argSymbol,MODE_ASK)," Ticket: ",CloseTicket);
            Print(ErrLog);
          }
        else Counter--;
      }
    }
  }


  void CloseAllBuyLimitOrders(string argSymbol, int argMagicNumber)
    {
      for(int Counter = 0; Counter <= OrdersTotal()-1; Counter++)
        {
          OrderSelect(Counter,SELECT_BY_POS);

          if(OrderMagicNumber() == argMagicNumber && OrderSymbol() == argSymbol
            && OrderType() == OP_BUYLIMIT)
            {
              // Delete Order
              int CloseTicket = OrderTicket();

              while(IsTradeContextBusy()) Sleep(10);

              bool Closed = OrderDelete(CloseTicket,Red);

              // Error Handling
              if(Closed == false)
                {
                  int ErrorCode = GetLastError();
                  string ErrDesc = ErrorDescription(ErrorCode);

                  string ErrAlert = StringConcatenate("Close All Buy Limit Orders - ",
                    "Error ",ErrorCode,": ",ErrDesc);
                  Alert(ErrAlert);

                  string ErrLog = StringConcatenate("Bid: ",
                    MarketInfo(argSymbol,MODE_BID)," Ask: ",
                    MarketInfo(argSymbol,MODE_ASK)," Ticket: ",CloseTicket);
                  Print(ErrLog);
                }
              else Counter--;
            }
        }
    }
```

```
void CloseAllSellLimitOrders(string argSymbol, int argMagicNumber)
  {
    for(int Counter = 0; Counter <= OrdersTotal()-1; Counter++)
      {
        OrderSelect(Counter,SELECT_BY_POS);

        if(OrderMagicNumber() == argMagicNumber && OrderSymbol() == argSymbol
          && OrderType() == OP_SELLLIMIT)
          {
            // Delete Order
            int CloseTicket = OrderTicket();

            while(IsTradeContextBusy()) Sleep(10);

            bool Closed = OrderDelete(CloseTicket,Red);

            // Error Handling
            if(Closed == false)
              {
                int ErrorCode = GetLastError();
                string ErrDesc = ErrorDescription(ErrorCode);

                string ErrAlert = StringConcatenate("Close All Sell Limit Orders - ",
                  "Error ",ErrorCode,": ",ErrDesc);
                Alert(ErrAlert);

                string ErrLog = StringConcatenate("Bid: ",
                  MarketInfo(argSymbol,MODE_BID)," Ask: ",
                  MarketInfo(argSymbol,MODE_ASK)," Ticket: ",CloseTicket);
                Print(ErrLog);
              }
            else Counter--;
          }
      }
  }


void BuyTrailingStop(string argSymbol, int argTrailingStop, int argMinProfit,
  int argMagicNumber)
  {
    for(int Counter = 0; Counter <= OrdersTotal()-1; Counter++)
      {
        OrderSelect(Counter,SELECT_BY_POS);

        // Calculate Max Stop and Min Profit
        double MaxStopLoss = MarketInfo(argSymbol,MODE_BID) -
          (argTrailingStop * PipPoint(argSymbol));

        MaxStopLoss = NormalizeDouble(MaxStopLoss,
          MarketInfo(OrderSymbol(),MODE_DIGITS));

        double CurrentStop = NormalizeDouble(OrderStopLoss(),
          MarketInfo(OrderSymbol(),MODE_DIGITS));
```

195

```
          double PipsProfit = MarketInfo(argSymbol,MODE_BID) - OrderOpenPrice();
          double MinProfit = argMinProfit * PipPoint(argSymbol);

          // Modify Stop
          if(OrderMagicNumber() == argMagicNumber && OrderSymbol() == argSymbol
            && OrderType() == OP_BUY && CurrentStop < MaxStopLoss
            && PipsProfit >= MinProfit)
            {
              bool Trailed = OrderModify(OrderTicket(),OrderOpenPrice(),MaxStopLoss,
                OrderTakeProfit(),0);

              // Error Handling
              if(Trailed == false)
                {
                  int ErrorCode = GetLastError();
                  string ErrDesc = ErrorDescription(ErrorCode);

                  string ErrAlert = StringConcatenate("Buy Trailing Stop – Error ",
                    ",ErrorCode,": ",ErrDesc);
                  Alert(ErrAlert);

                  string ErrLog = StringConcatenate("Bid: ",
                    MarketInfo(argSymbol,MODE_BID)," Ticket: ",OrderTicket()," Stop: ",
                    OrderStopLoss()," Trail: ",MaxStopLoss);
                  Print(ErrLog);
                }
            }
        }
    }


void SellTrailingStop(string argSymbol, int argTrailingStop, int argMinProfit,
  int argMagicNumber)
  {
    for(int Counter = 0; Counter <= OrdersTotal()-1; Counter++)
      {
        OrderSelect(Counter,SELECT_BY_POS);

        // Calculate Max Stop and Min Profit
        double MaxStopLoss = MarketInfo(argSymbol,MODE_ASK) +
          (argTrailingStop * PipPoint(argSymbol));

        MaxStopLoss = NormalizeDouble(MaxStopLoss,
          MarketInfo(OrderSymbol(),MODE_DIGITS));

        double CurrentStop = NormalizeDouble(OrderStopLoss(),
          MarketInfo(OrderSymbol(),MODE_DIGITS));

        double PipsProfit = OrderOpenPrice() - MarketInfo(argSymbol,MODE_ASK);
        double MinProfit = argMinProfit * PipPoint(argSymbol);
```

```
// Modify Stop
if(OrderMagicNumber() == argMagicNumber && OrderSymbol() == argSymbol
   && OrderType() == OP_SELL && (CurrentStop > MaxStopLoss || CurrentStop == 0)
   && PipsProfit >= MinProfit)
  {
    bool Trailed = OrderModify(OrderTicket(),OrderOpenPrice(),MaxStopLoss,
      OrderTakeProfit(),0);

    // Error Handling
    if(Trailed == false)
      {
        int ErrorCode = GetLastError();
        string ErrDesc = ErrorDescription(ErrorCode);

        string ErrAlert = StringConcatenate("Sell Trailing Stop - Error ",
          ErrorCode,": ",ErrDesc);
        Alert(ErrAlert);

        string ErrLog = StringConcatenate("Ask: ",
          MarketInfo(argSymbol,MODE_ASK)," Ticket: ",OrderTicket()," Stop: ",
          OrderStopLoss()," Trail: ",MaxStopLoss);
        Print(ErrLog);
      }
  }
}
}
```

Appendix E

Custom Indicator

Here is the code for the custom indicator from chapter 9:

```
#property copyright "Andrew Young"

#property indicator_chart_window
#property indicator_buffers 3
#property indicator_color1 DeepSkyBlue
#property indicator_color2 DeepSkyBlue
#property indicator_color3 DeepSkyBlue


// External variables
extern int BandsPeriod = 20;
extern int BandsShift = 0;
extern int BandsMethod = 1;
extern int BandsPrice = 0;
extern int Deviations = 1;


// Buffers
double EMA[];
double UpperBand[];
double LowerBand[];


// Init
int init()
  {
    SetIndexStyle(0,DRAW_LINE);
    SetIndexBuffer(0,EMA);
    SetIndexLabel(0,"EMA");

    SetIndexStyle(1,DRAW_LINE);
    SetIndexBuffer(1,UpperBand);
    SetIndexLabel(1,"UpperBand");

    SetIndexStyle(2,DRAW_LINE);
    SetIndexBuffer(2,LowerBand);
    SetIndexLabel(2,"LowerBand");

    return(0);
  }
```